Persis M. Breed
Christmas 1937.

From
Marion B. Barron

TRINITY CHURCH

TRINITY CHURCH

COLUMBIA, S. C.

ONE HUNDRED AND TWENTY-FIFTH ANNIVERSARY

1937

1937
THE STATE COMPANY
COLUMBIA, S. C.

CONTENTS

ILLUSTRATIONS

FOREWORD

August 12, 1937 was the one hundred and twenty-fifth anniversary of Trinity Church. In the spring of last year this fact was brought before the vestry.

The vestry authorized the appointment of a committee to bring the matter before the congregation at the annual congregational meeting in January, 1937. The members of the committee were Robert Moorman, Mrs. T. H. Fisher and Miss Louly Shand.

Records of the parish were destroyed in 1865. Had it not been that the 50th anniversary of Dr. Shand's rectorate was made the occasion for gathering the history of the parish, all the story of its early days would have been lost. It is now fitting to mark the one hundred and twenty-fifth anniversary and to make it the occasion for collecting and putting into permanent form the history of the parish from all available records and from the recollections of those now living.

At the congregational meeting, the report of the committee as appointed was adopted as follows:

1. That this year the one hundred and twenty-fifth anniversary be celebrated in a simple, dignified, but impressive way;

2. That all members of the congregation be urged to renew their faith and reconsecrate themselves at the time of the celebration of the Holy Communion as planned by the Rector;

3. That all records and recollections available be gathered together and put in permanent form, for the benefit of all members of the congregation but especially for the new and younger members;

4. That the records of our historic old churchyard form a part of this history; and

5. That the Rector appoint a committee of five, with himself as chairman, to make arrangements for all details of the celebration of this anniversary.

Henry D. Phillips.

Rector.

COMMITTEE ON ARRANGEMENTS

In accord with the resolutions of the Congregation the following committee was appointed to act with the Rector: the Senior Warden, William E. Gonzales; the Junior Warden, Carroll H. Jones; President of the Daughters of the Holy Cross, Mrs. W. Bedford Moore, Jr.; and Past President of the Daughters of the Holy Cross, Mrs. Morris C. Lumpkin. As the anniversary fell during the month of August, the committee set the time for the official observance as November 19-21.

The offering, which will be in the nature of a birthday offering, is to commemorate and symbolize the Commission of our Lord, to preach the Gospel throughout the world and to teach in His Name. Therefore, the two objects of the offering of the parish are, the missionary work at the Hudson Stuck Memorial Hospital at Fort Yukon, Alaska, under the direction of Dr. Grafton Burke; and the Christian education carried on by the University of the South at Sewanee, Tenn.

Every member of the congregation is asked to make his or her expression of thanksgiving and personal dedication at one of the services of the celebration of the Holy Communion on Sunday, November 21.

The preacher at the mid-day service will be the Rt. Rev. Kirkman G. Finlay, D. D., Bishop of the Diocese of Upper South Carolina, who with the exception of the present Rector, the Rev. Henry D. Phillips, D. D., is the only living Rector of Trinity parish.

The members of the committee were assigned special work. The Rector was to arrange for the services; the Senior Warden to arrange for editing the records and history of the parish; the Junior Warden to be in charge of the publication; and the presidents of the Daughters of the Holy Cross to arrange for the reception of the congregation on Friday.

The committee appointed the following to gather information for the publication: the Parish, Robert Moorman; the Church School, Mrs. H. L. Forbes; the Parish House, William M. Shand; Women's Work, Miss Louly Shand; Men's Work, Kirkman Finlay; Gifts and Memorials, Mrs. T. H. Fisher; Churchyard, Mrs. Artemus E. Legare; Wardens and Vestrymen, R. E. Carwile; Communicants, Miss Roberta Aldrich. The committee is very much indebted to Mrs. Henry L. Forbes for painstaking care in editing the publication and enriching the facts and accounts which were gathered by those who worked so industriously to make the record complete.

In setting forth the work and life of the parish there are bound to be omissions, but all who have made contributions have striven to make the account as complete and as accurate as possible.

HISTORY OF TRINITY CHURCH

I

FOUNDING AND EARLY YEARS

1812-1860

Columbia was founded in 1786; but some thirty years before, while South Carolina was still an English colony, at least a plan had been considered to plant the Church of England, established religion of the Province since 1706, in the inland regions. The General Assembly of the Province, in 1756, appropriated 700 pounds per annum to pay a minister of the Established Church to perform divine services at Saxe Gotha, "or such other centrical places in the Congarees," within forty miles of Saxe Gotha, which territory embraced the site of Columbia.[1]

No record is found of such services having been performed or of any congregation of our Church organized in Saxe Gotha territory earlier than 1812.

In a sermon delivered February 10, 1884, at the semi-centennial celebration of Dr. Peter J. Shand's rectorship of Trinity church, the Rev. Robert Wilson, D. D., said:

"On the 8th day of August, 1812, the first organization of the Church in Columbia was accomplished by the action of a meeting composed of John G. and James S. Guignard, Edward Fisher, Benjamin R. Waring, Robert Stark, William Harper, Theodore Gaillard, William Branthwaite, Warren R. Davis, Samuel Percival and William Marshall."

This group enlisted the interest of the Protestant Episcopal Society for the Advancement of Christianity in South Carolina, and the Society sent here as a missionary, the Rev. Andrew Fowler. He conducted in 1812, in the original State House, the first Protestant Episcopal service in Columbia.

Of the founding of Trinity Church in Columbia, the following from Dalcho's history of the church in this state is informing:

"Columbia was founded by Act of Assembly, 1786, and established as the seat of government of the State. In 1812, the Protestant Episcopal Society sent the Rev. Mr. Fowler as their Missionary to this town. He arrived there July 16, and by the 5th of October, 'he had collected a considerable congregation,

[1]Frederick Dalcho, M. D., "Protestant Episcopal Church in South Carolina (1820), page 460, Art. VIII.

composed of very respectable members of the community, who appeared to attend public worship with great devotion, and seemed to be zealous that all things should be done decently and in order."[2] Mr. Fowler was greatly aided by the active cooperation of some zealous and respectable individuals, through whose influence a congregation was collected. In 1814, a neat and commodious Church was built of wood, by the liberality of several persons, in various parts of the State, and was consecrated by the late Bishop Dehon. The Rev. Mr. Lance (Maurice Harvey), while preparing for the Ministry, officiated in this Church, as a Lay-Reader under the license of the Bishop, and was supported by an apppropriation of the Society.

"Gen. Wade Hampton generously made the Church a donation of an Organ, and upwards of $2,000. The Legislature of 1813,[3] Gen. C. C. Pinckney, Elias Horry and Peter Smith, Esqrs. of Charleston, have endowed it with lands. Mrs. Mary Gregorie and Mrs. Sarah Russell, of Charleston, have likewise contributed to its adornment; and Elias Lynch Horry, Esq., of Charleston, presented it with the Communion plate, consisting of a Flagon, Chalice, and Paten. The present Incumbent, the Rev. Christian Hanckell, has been their only Minister. He was appointed November 29, 1815, Professor of Mathematics and Natural Philosophy in the So. Car. College, but in consequence of a late and judicious regulation, of the Trustees, prohibiting the Professors from holding parochial cures, he will soon retire from the College, and devote himself entirely to the pastoral office. As the burden of his support will then fall solely upon his Church, whose means, as yet, are small, the Protestant Episcopal Society have generously appropriated $1,000 per annum for three years, in aid of their funds for the support of the Minister, so soon as his connexion with the College shall cease."

The Church was Incorporated in 1813, by the name of "the Protestant Episcopal Church in Columbia.[4]

---

[2]Third Report of the P. E. Society for Advancement of Christianity in South Carolina.

[3]Tenth Report of the Board of Trustees of the same society.

[4]Statutes of South Carolina, page 268: Act of Incorporation in full:

XVI. AND BE IT ENACTED by the authority aforesaid, That the Episcopal Church of Columbia, and the several persons who now are, or shall hereafter be, and they are hereby declared to be, a body corporate, in deed and in name, by the name and style of "The Protestant Episcopal Church in Columbia;" and by the said name, shall have perpetual succession of officers and members, and a common seal, with power to alter, change, break and make new the same, as often as said corporation shall judge expedient. And the said corporation shall be able and capable in law, to purchase, have, hold, receive, enjoy, possess and retain, to itself, in perpetuity or for any term of years, any estate or estates, goods, chattels, lands or tenements, of what kind or nature soever, not exceeding the sum of ten thousand dollars; and to sell, alien, exchange, demise or lease the same, or any part thereof, as they shall think proper; and may, by the said name, sue and be sued, implead and be impleaded, answer and be answered unto, in any court of law or equity in this State. And the Wardens and Vestry of the said church are hereby vested with all the powers and authorities which are vested in any established Episcopal church in this State.

The Legislature of South Carolina, in 1813, passed an Act in which will be found the following language:

"And be it enacted by the authority aforesaid, that the balance of monies arising from the sale of two acres of land, originally destined as sites for places of public worship, but lately disposed of for the purpose of purchasing land in a situation better adapted for a public burial ground, after completing the payments on said purchase, shall be equally divided between the following four named religious societies, viz.: the Protestant Episcopal church, the Presbyterian, Baptist and Methodist congregations of the town of Columbia, for the benefit and use of the said named congregations, forever."[5]

This same Act also provided:

"That the lots Nos. 37, 38, 39, and 40, being the one-half of the old burying ground in the Town of Columbia, be appraised by Col. Thomas Taylor, Judge Gaillard and Judge DeSaussure, and as soon as such appraisement shall be made, the Intendant and Wardens of the said Town, are authorized and are hereby required to convey the said lots to the First Presbyterian Church in the Town of Columbia, and to The Protestant Episcopal Church in said Town, and their successors in office forever, for the purpose of erecting churches thereon, and the said appraisers aforesaid are hereby required to divide the said lots between the said Churches in equal proportions, in such manner as in their opinion will be most advantageous to the said Churches, for the purposes aforesaid; Provided nevertheless, and it is hereby enacted, that before the title shall be executed so as aforesaid, the said First Presbyterian Church, and the said Protestant Episcopal Church, shall pay to the Methodist and Baptist Churches established in the said Town, the one-half of the sum to which said lots shall be appraised as aforesaid, to be equally divided between them, for the purpose of enabling them to finish and complete their said Churches."[6]

But this was not all. The General Assembly of 1814 authorized and empowered wardens and vestry of our church to conduct a lottery to raise money, not exceeding $2,000, "for the use, benefit and support of the said Church."[7] No authentic record can be found to show that the vestry of the "zealous and respectable congregation" as reported by the missionaries of the Advancement Society, ever availed themselves of this privilege. The act granted the same privilege to the First Presbyterian Church of Columbia also.

---

[5]Statutes of South Carolina, Vol. VIII, page 266.
[6]Ibid., pages 268, 269.

It is not certain how our parish acquired the two acres upon which stand our house of worship and our cemetery and upon which our new parish house was built, because the records of conveyances of this county were destroyed by fire started by General Sherman's soldiers in February 1865. However, the tradition is that the northern acre was given by a widow Smythe in 1813, and that the southern acre was purchased from Col. James Gregg in 1814. Mrs. Smythe's gift was coupled with the idea that she and her family should be buried under the magnificent live-oak tree in our burying ground. It seems that by mistake someone else was buried where Mrs. Smythe desired to be buried and this provoked her to such an extent that she withdrew from the congregation. She and her family are buried elsewhere.

Col. Gregg sold his acre upon the condition that no graves should be dug thereon, and that condition has been faithfully performed. Col. Gregg lived at No. 1310 Senate street, just opposite to and south of the churchyard. Evidently he did not wish to look from his home upon a grave yard. This southern acre was the lot where Col. Gregg kept his animals and where at one time he butchered his hogs. Col. Gregg was a distinguished lawyer of the early Columbia bar.

In 1813, Trinity church, Columbia, was represented in the Diocesan Council, meeting, as it almost always did in the early days in one of the Charleston churches, by Charles Kershaw and Robert Hazelhurst,[8] probably proxies or non-resident delegates, allowed as a concession to the difficulties of a journey from the hinterlands to "the City."

At this Council, Bishop Dehon reported:[9]

"The congregation of Episcopalians in Columbia, collected and organized under the labors of a missionary of the Protestant Episcopal Society, have, with the aid of donations for the work from many zealous and benevolent individuals of the community, finished arrangements for the erection in that place of a building for the purpose of Christian worship according to the usages of our Church."

The corner-stone of this church was laid on the 7th day of March, 1814, and the building was consecrated by Bishop Dehon, December 14, 1814, under the name of "Trinity Church."[10]

[7]Statutes of South Carolina, Volume V, page 725.
[8]Journal of Diocese, 1813, from Dalcho.
[9]Ibid.
[10]Journal of Diocese, 1814, from Dalcho.

The first parochial report of Trinity, Columbia, was presented to the 25th Diocesan council in 1813. The report made then by Rev. Andrew Fowler, minister-in-charge, showed 11 communicants, 4 baptisms, one adult, 3 children.

On December 7 and 8, 1815, the Convention of the Diocese met at Trinity, Columbia, in the newly completed church, of which Bishop Dehon made reference thus in his address to the Council:

"It is pleasant to find the Convention assembled this year in a place where, but a few years ago, the worship of our Church had been unheard and her character in great measure unknown. While we witness the success which has attained the efforts to establish a Church in Columbia, amidst circumstances by no means propitious to the accomplishment of such a purpose, what encouragement should be derived from it to make perseveringly efforts for similar ends in places where the Church once existed, but is now desolate.

"It is true that in the erection of this goodly temple, and in the establishment of the society which so happily worships in it, there have been some notable acts of individual and private beneficence, and it ought to be known to the Churches, for the benefit which such examples are calculated to produce, that, besides other endowments from other quarters, there were given by one gentleman of this neighborhood, General Wade Hampton, nearly $3,000 to the treasury of the work which we see here accomplished."

Representatives of Trinity at this convention were the first Rector, Rev. Christian Hanckel, and Theodore Gaillard, John Spencer Man, and Edward Fisher.

Ambitious and hospitable indeed this young congregation in "the Congarees;" communicants that year numbered "about 30 whites and one black."

Of this first church building, Robert W. Shand, son of Dr. Peter J. Shand, wrote:

"I well remember the wooden cruciform Trinity Church, which I attended. It stood in the North-west corner of the present Church yard; and its pews, as before that time was common, were, some oblong, as is now universal in churches, and some square or nearly so; which required in a full pew, some of the worshippers to sit with their sides, and some with their backs to the officiating minister. When the new (present structure) church was erected in the late forties, the old church was sold to a purchaser who bound himself to remove it. The purchaser if I remember aright was Mr. Alexander Herbemont. But I know that the building was torn down, and the material used in the construction of the large dwelling house on the lot where now stands the McMaster School. The house so built passed in late years to the ownership of Elias Cain, by whom it was moved to the East side of Henderson Street between College and Green."

By 1817 the "about 30" had fallen off; communicants that year were listed at 23 whites, 1 black; but in general the congregation continued to increase. Mr. Hanckel served until 1818, and was succeeded by the Rev. H. P. Folker.

Little is known of his pastorate. No parochial reports from Trinity appear in the Diocean journals for several years. He served as Rector until 1824, and was succeeded by the Rev. Thomas S. W. Motte. Again, records are lacking of parish activities of that day. The Rev. Mr. Motte was Rector until approximately 1830.

For a while the parish was without a rector. Then young Peter Shand, who gave up the law to study for the ministry, began serving as lay-reader. After his ordination he became Rector, assuming this office, January 26, 1834. He served as Rector of Trinity parish until his death on November 1, 1886.

Immediately reports began going in to the Diocesan secretary from Trinity. In 1836, Dr. Shand's first report, showed 48 communicants and 68 non-communicant members.[11]

In the parish report of 1842 is the interesting fact that "between $500 and $600 was received and remitted to the Domestic and Foreign Missionary Society of the Church at New York." "Contributions as usual" were made to the Bishop's Fund, to the Advancement Society, and a "small sum" for Diocesan missions.

The original church edifice was now becoming too small, and thoughts of the congregation turned toward building a new one. Advantages of the site chosen, almost in the center of the church property, can be seen today. To the north lies the cemetery, to the south the parish house and the wide lawn. The church is surrounded by the space necessary to keep its graceful lines cleancut, its fine proportions in good perspective.

The year 1846 is important in the history of the parish. In this year the corner-stone of the present church building was

---

[11]Statistics here and hereafter in this sketch of the Parish unless otherwise noted are from Journals of the Diocese of South Carolina, and, after 1923, Journals of Diocese of Upper South Carolina.

THE CHANCEL, TRINITY CHURCH

laid, and the edifice was consecrated to the worship of Almighty God by Bishop Gadsden on February 14, 1847.

It is said that the Hampton family alone offered to build this church, but that the wise Rector, Dr. Shand, insisted that the funds be raised by popular subscription. This was done. Probably the Hamptons contributed liberally, but the building was the embodiment of the desires and the work of the congregation as a whole.

George Waring declares that his father, Clark Waring, then a lad of about 19 years, was a foreman or superintendent in the building of the Church in 1846. It is an interesting coincidence that among the founders of the parish was a Waring (Benjamin), that among the builders of our present church was a Waring (Clark) and that in 1937, as the 125th anniversary of the parish is celebrated, there is on the vestry of the parish a Waring (Clark).

It is estimated by an experienced contractor of today[12] that the cost of the building in 1846, then without transepts, and excepting the windows, altar, pulpit, pews, and so forth, was about $12,000. Probably the $3,000 bequeathed to Dr. Shand, as Rector by Mrs. Mary Parr was used in the erection of this building.

Nearly all of the stained glass windows are originals, including the very beautiful rose windows, and all were presented by the Preston family. These windows came from Munich. A few of the originals have been replaced by memorials.

The late Robert W. Shand wrote, concerning the erection of the building:

"The new (present) Trinity Church is a copy of Yorkminster, in England, but of reduced size.

"Mr. E. E. White of Charleston was the architect, and when visiting his work during its progress was guest at my father's house. . . . The two transepts of the church as it now stands were not in the original construction, but were added in 1861-62."

Richland county records were destroyed in 1865. But it appears that the original rectory was at the southwest corner of the intersection of Sumter and Senate streets. The Arthur Moore map of Columbia made about 1850 shows a plat of about two acres bounded by Senate, Sumter and Pendleton streets, in the name of "Episcopal Church." Here a frame building housed Dr. Shand and his family.

---

[12]Geo. Waring, son of Clark Waring, foreman on the building.

In the year 1856 in assessments on the parishes for the Bishop's fund Trinity's assignment was $50, this being as large as that of any church outside of Charleston. This year, and again in 1860, Dr. Shand was elected deputy to the General Convention of the Church.

Trinity was now one of the largest of the parishes outside the old churches of the Low-Country. Its membership numbered 126 communicants and 137 non-communicants. That year the gift of the parish to diocesan missions was $114.03, for domestic missions $353.15; "Total contributions" $1,288.63. A parochial school was conducted by private subscriptions.

II

War's Destruction and Post-War Growth

1860-1917

Breaking into this steady march of progress and growth in Trinity parish was the War between the States. Columbia, capital of the State which lead in the Secession movement, was fervidly and passionately in harmony with the State; the members of the congregation of Trinity parish were ardent in their support of the Southern cause. At once the congregation was affected. The church was bled of its manhood and its means. The leaden covering of the finials on the church, it is said, went into bullets for the Confederate army.

At first, however, while hope of victory was still high, the parish courageously embarked on a building program, adding the transepts in 1861-62. During building operations, the congregation met for worship in the "new university chapel"[13] (building at Green and Sumter streets now used as gymnasium).

As the war went on the city filled up with refugees from the Low-Country, and the congregation, especially the ladies, had their hands full helping strangers in the city, besides working indefatigably to carry on their homes and to make and contribute supplies for the army. At least some of the refugee families from the coast stayed on in Columbia after the war and became valuable members of the parish.

At Trinity, during the war, was held a meeting of representatives of Southern dioceses to consider separation of the Ameri-

---

[13]Journal of the Diocese of South Carolina, 1862.

can Church into Northern and Southern branches. Happily the catholic spirit of the Church prevailed and no formal division took place.

Of course, however, prayers were offered in Trinity for the Confederacy and for the president of the Southern federation. It is told of "un-Reconstructed Rebels" of the congregation that when prayers for the president of the United States were once more read, here and there over the church heads would bob up as the owners sat up stiff and straight while petitions for the health and happiness of the "Yankee" president went up.

That the tragedy of war swept through the parish with heart-breaking results is evidenced by the long list of war dead, their names inscribed on a bronze tablet on the south wall of the church.

When the city was burned on the night of February 17, 1865, Dr. Shand in fear for the church, took the plate and the church records to the rectory with him. Writing of that dreadful night in Columbia, the Rev. Robert Wilson, son-in-law of Dr. Shand, wrote on March 1, 1865, to R. W. Shand:

"Your father's (the Rev. Dr. Shand's) life was threatened twice, and his trunk was taken away with his sermons and the church plate. The latter is gone, but some of the former have been found. . . . The house was destroyed and everything in it."

"Everything" included the records of the church since its founding in 1812.

Providentially the church building was spared, though Union soldiers rode rough-shod through the churchyard, and the Sunday school building was burned.

The church windows, tradition says, had been taken out and hidden, thus escaping destruction.

The bleakness of the years following immediately upon the burning of the city and the collapse a few months later of the Confederacy, was little more than most of the South endured. With courage every whit as great as that of the soldiers who fought for the Lost Cause, the people of Columbia and of Trinity parish gathered up the shattered fragments of their old life and built anew.

At the Diocesan Council held in 1867, no report was made of communicants, but the Rector made the following report:

"Divine Services were held on Festivals and Fast days. Owing to heavy debt due by the church and the almost universal impoverishment of the congregation, there have been no collections made during the year, except for the poor and destitute of the parish; the people haven't recovered, except in a very limited measure, from the Sack and Conflagration in February 18, 1865."

In 1869, in this post-war depression, the parish conveyed to George Trenholm of Charleston for $14,000 Confederate money, the "parsonage lot," in consideration of $14,000 in Confederate currency lent to the church in May, 1863 by John Fraser & Co., of Charleston; this conveyance of the property cancelling the obligation of the loan. (Perhaps a loan in connection with the addition of the transepts to the church building).[14] In this transaction is recorded use of a new seal of Trinity church, the old one having been lost or destroyed.

On January 15, 1870, M. LaBorde, chairman of wardens and vestry, bought back from George Trenholm, obviously for Trinity parish, one-half acre of the old rectory lot; the lot purchased measuring 104 feet, 4 inches on Senate and 208 feet, 8 inches on Sumter street. The price was $1,250, good United States money.

That summer and fall a two-story frame building was erected to serve as the rectory.[15] The cost was $3,775. It appears from minutes of vestry meetings, that the vestry had some difficulty in paying, but did shortly remove the debt on that building.

In 1876, year of destiny for South Carolina, when Hampton led and Red Shirts rode, the congregation of Trinity entertained the Diocesan Council again. Dr. Shand reported "the whole number of souls" in his cure was 411, of whom 234 were communicants. Sixty dollars was paid to the Bishop's Fund, and a parochial school of 70 pupils and three teachers was in operation, maintained by volunteer subscriptions and workers from the parish.

The Rev. J. H. Stringfellow was assistant to Dr. Shand from 1874 to 1878. Then Rev. H. O. Judd became the assistant, and served in this capacity until the death of Dr. Shand.

The city as well as the parish was coming back slowly from the ruin of 1864-65. As from its founding even to the present, the town drew from other sections of the state. Some were Episcopalians. Mr. Judd, feeling that another congregation of

---

[14]Richland County deed recorded in Clerk's office; Book P, page 609.
[15]Contract recorded in Deed Book F, page 101.

PARISH HOUSE AND CHURCH—SNOW SCENE

the Church would serve them more conveniently, began in 1883 holding services in a residence in the northeastern section of the city. At the Diocesan Council, meeting at Trinity again in 1885, there was presented a report from the "Chapel of the Good Shepherd, recent outgrowth of Trinity Parish."

This daughter of Trinity is now a fine, sturdy congregation worshipping in a beautiful church edifice on Blanding street, its communicants numbering 500; and preparing to celebrate in 1888 the 50th anniversary of its admission as a parish. Further, this congregation and its ministers have to their credit the establishment of two other parishes in the city, St. Timothy's and St. John's.

Only an incident in the Church's building program, but an interesting sidelight on the mode of life in that day, is the record of the erection in the early summer of 1884, of "six hitching posts around the church grounds," and carrying of the city water pipes into the churchyard.

Those hitching posts, as many members still recall, were iron posts some three to four feet in height, capped with horses' heads. Through their mouths ran the iron rings to which drivers of buggies and horseback riders fastened their reins to hold their horses while the owners went in to service. Used also by every Sunday school child for nearly two generations as swinging posts. These iron horses and the large stone carriage-block at the main entrance and the smaller ones at the side gates were removed when street paving changed the line of the sidewalk. Of a piece with these in their flavor of a bygone day are the iron mud-scrapers still standing by the church steps, designed for those who trod bravely through the muddy streets of the little town of Columbia to attend church in bad weather.

Dr. Shand's long connection with Trinity, his long service to church, community and state, came to an end with his death on November 1, 1886, after a rectorate of fifty-two years. Years of building and growth, years of dreadful loss and destruction, hard years of rebuilding.

The congregation was plunged into grief at this parting with their leader, guide and loving shepherd of more than a half century. The church was draped in mourning for thirty days, and resolutions expressing the sorrow of the congregation were adopted. Later, as a memorial to Dr. Shand, the window now in place above the altar was installed, the funds for this being raised by general contributions from the whole congregation.

He was the "grand old man" of this congregation, and all the members of Trinity should always revere his memory. He not only gave nearly all of his noble life to the upbuilding of Trinity as an important factor in the plan of salvation, but he left to this church a family that has continued his splendid work. It would be embarrassing to them to state what the Shands have done for Trinity and for this city and even beyond its limits. For nearly one hundred years this family of nature's nobility have wielded a powerful influence for good.

During Dr. Shand's long rectorship Trinity grew from about thirty communicants to about 350, and completely outgrew the original church building and also the second as originally built.

Shortly after Dr. Shand's death Mr. Judd became Rector. His connection with the parish was cut short by failing health, and he left the parish in 1887.

The Rev. Ellison Capers, D.D., assuming the rectorship in 1887, was the tender, loving minister until his consecration as Bishop in 1893.

The annual report of 1892 gives a glimpse of the parish in his rectorate:

Families 136; communicants 309; Sunday school, 13 teachers, 145 pupils. Parochial school 5 teachers and 80 pupils.

"Working societies" of Trinity were "Church Aid Society, which assists the Rector in aiding the poor; Trinity branch of the Woman's Auxiliary; the Church Adornment Society, the Shand Chapter of the Brotherhood of St. Andrew," all reported active.

In 1893 the question of wiring the church for electric lights was considered; but the gas lights which flickered and flared from wall brackets and from the pillars in the nave continued to furnish "dim religious" light for a good many more years.

The consecration of Bishop Capers took place in Trinity church July 20, 1893. *The State* of the next day described the service as the "grandest religious ceremony ever witnessed here."

Dr. William E. Evans began his seven years' rectorate in 1893. This was a period filled with material and spiritual development in the parish. Perhaps the most valuable contribution Dr. Evans made to Trinity and to Columbia was the mobilizing of the womanhood of his parish into active enthusiastic groups, The Guild and the Daughters of the Holy Cross. The parish has been immeasurably strengthened by their work and ideals.

To the Diocesan Council, meeting in 1894, at Trinity, Dr. Evans reported 332 communicants.

Dr. Evans accepted a call to a Virginia parish in 1900. Following him as Rector of Trinity was the Rev. Churchill Satterlee of beloved memory. A gentleman of beautiful Christian humility, of warm missionary spirit, and withal of exceptional charm and friendliness.

Particularly interested in the problem of spiritual care for the many souls gathering in the newly rising industrial centers of the South, he organized a mission in the Olympia mill district, just south of Columbia. Quick to follow his lead, the congregation of Trinity and the mill authorities cooperated whole-heartedly. Through contributions from the parish and from outside sources, he built up a fine community work in this district, erecting a chapel, and a mission-house with a deaconess in charge. Trinity Mission still carries on with a clergyman and a United Thank offering worker staffing it.

The Rev. Mr. Satterlee began plans for a new Sunday school building for the parish, but these did not materialize during his brief ministry. His death in 1904 cut short a useful and beautiful life.

Bishop Capers, at the annual council of the Diocese in May, 1904, paid this tribute to him:

"Mr. Satterlee took charge of Trinity Church, Columbia, in January, 1901, coming to us from Morganton, N. C., though a native of New York. His rectorship of Trinity had been for the brief period of three years and a few days, yet those three years had been so wholly given to his work, and were such telling witnesses before the community and his people, of his consecration and energy, his self-effacement and godly love, that I have never known a clergyman more universally esteemed in any community, or more respected and beloved in a parish than was our departed brother. Brief as it was, his ministry was a marked success, and its spiritual impress will remain with his people. St. Luke's tribute to the ministry of Barnabas at Antioch was true of Satterlee's ministry in Columbia: 'For he was a good man, and full of the Holy Ghost and of faith; and much people was added unto the Lord.'"

Shortly after the death of the Rev. Churchill Satterlee, the Rev. Charles Martin Niles, D. D., was called to Trinity from a parish in New York state. His was a vigorous personality, and he pushed plans for the erection of a parish house. The building known as Satterlee Hall, in memory of the Rev. Churchill Satterlee, was one unit of the plan for a far larger building. Satterlee Hall was put into use in 1907. Serving as assistant to Dr. Niles and in charge of Trinity Mission for about two years was Rev. Samuel Moran.

Dr. Niles, of a school of churchmanship different from that prevailing in the South, advocated material changes in the chancel and the altar, and elaborations of the ritual not altogether acceptable here. He secured for the parish a very handsome altar with a reredos. This was installed, but against the wishes of a militant minority. Unhappy were the fruits of the very definite split which developed in the congregation on this issue.

Dr. Niles resigned in 1907. The reredos was removed and stored in the basement of the church. With its removal and Dr. Niles' departure; but more especially under the quiet, tactful spirit of the new Rector, the Rev. Kirkman G. Finlay, the congregation drew together again.

The Rev. William Alexander Guerry, D. D., who was elected Bishop Coadjutor of South Carolina at the Diocesan Council meeting at Trinity, Columbia in May, 1907, was consecrated Bishop in the same church, September 15, 1907.

The Rev. Mr. Finlay refused to be drawn into the controversy which had centered around Dr. Niles and the reredos. That piece of marble, the new Rector is reported to have said, was the tombstone of one man's career at Trinity; it should not be his.

In the something over thirteen years of Mr. Finlay's rectorship the parish grew in size, but marked even greater growth in certain spiritual intangibles; and in the strengthening of democratic principles of parish administration.

There was notable development of missionary spirit. In 1907 when Mr. Finlay took charge of the congregation, contributions to Diocesan and general missions amounted to approximately $1,500.00. In the last year of his rectorship, 1921, they totaled $12,500.00.[16]

---

[16]Treasurer's Reports 1907 and 1921.

REV. PETER J. SHAND, D. D.
Rector, 1834-1886

There grew up, too, intense zeal for social causes, with corresponding spreading of the influence of the parish in the community. Record of the women's work reflects this particularly in the beginning of the anti-tuberculosis work of the Daughters of the Holy Cross, the successful beginning and conduct of the Woman's Exchange, work for the Rescue Orphanage, the Door of Hope, and enlarged activities in charity work in general.

A minor social and a major financial revolution was accomplished under this Rector's leadership, in the long-considered abolition of rented pews and the institution of the Every Member Canvass as chief source of parish support.

Strongly rooted in the old aristocracy of the Church in the Low-Country, Trinity followed the ways of those parishes in many respects. It adopted without hesitation the almost universal custom of that day in the matter of renting pews.

Pew rents were the main support of the parish for generations; but were not an altogether satisfactory source of income. In the poverty of the post-war years, many found it difficult to pay rent, yet were too proud to sit in "free pews", so labeled with large bronze markers. When rents were in arrears, dunning the renters was unpleasant, collecting sometimes impossible. Pews under such circumstances were expected to be declared "Vacant", and advertised for rent.

Was this the spirit of the free Gospel of Christ?

Again, rented pews, especially old-fashioned pews with doors, did not invite strangers to enter. An occasional pew-renter, too, had the feeling that the pew was his; anyone other than his family entering it did so only when he opened the door and gave the invitation.

It was not long after the Confederate war that these points began to bob up in vestry meetings and in congregational meetings too. There was a further undemocratic principle involved; only renters of pews could vote, and even this excepted female pew-holders. Under this system but a small proportion of members of the parish had voice in the conduct of its affairs. In 1907, for example there were 80 pew-holders, 14 of them women; and 436 communicants.

Back in the 80's the vestry discussed these evils. In the 90's they continued to discuss them. There arose advocates of the then almost revolutionary idea of free pews. In 1894, as concession to these, pews were made free at afternoon and evening services. Pews were provided always for the Rector and for certain other families and for students.

As stated, the question of suffrage was closely linked with the free pew issue. Mr. Finlay was an outspoken advocate of free pews, support of the parish by voluntary contributions and votes for all adult members of the parish.

In 1909, at the annual congregational meeting, resolutions were adopted giving the vote to every adult communicant of the parish. This action, involving change of the by-laws, called for ratification by the next succeeding congregational meeting.

On March 28, 1910,[17] the congregational meeting gave this confirmation, thus extending privileges of the vote in parish affairs to men and women of the congregation, regardless of whether they were pew-renters or not. It is interesting to note that this was nine years before the vote was granted to South Carolina women in civic matters by the operation of the 19th Amendment to the Constitution of the United States.

Logical development of the freeing of the pews was the institution of the Every Member Canvass.

The yeast of democracy worked slowly; too, the uncertainty of income from the untried method of support by pledges balked the progressives. Gradually, there came to be a number of persons who pledged sums to the parish independently of pew rents. A small number of pew-holders were among these. As early as 1899 there were pledges made to supplement pew rents.

Finally, after some delays, some warm feeling, and some doubts—the issue carried through several years at congregational meetings—pews were declared free in Trinity parish, and the Every Member Canvass endorsed. This was in the congregational meeting of March 24, 1913.[18] Thus the second and third of the Rector's liberal measures went into effect.

[17]This condensed account of the movement for free pews is based on facts taken from minutes of vestry and congregational meetings dating from 1883 on; and from traditions and recollections of members of the parish.

Minutes of Congregational meeting, March 28, 1910: "Confirmed action of former meeting (1909) to extend right of vote to all adult communicants of the church whose names were on the parish roll for 12 months previous to a meeting."

[18]Meeting of congregation, March 24, 1913, Minute: "Adopted the following resolution: 'Be it resolved that the existing system of renting pews as one of the means of raising funds for the budget of the parish, be and the same hereby is abolished, and that hereafter the system of pledges and cash offerings from all of the worshippers in the church be adopted and relied upon as the means of providing such funds."

"A motion to table was defeated.

"By motion the vestry was requested to carry out the purposes of the above resolution."

The first canvass, conducted almost immediately after this historic meeting of the congregation was a pronounced success. When the men met to begin the canvass it was found that 100 per cent of the canvassers, 60 men, were present. From then on, the parish of Trinity has been supported by the pledges of a large proportion of its membership, these pledges made at the time of the annual Every Member Canvass. At the same time pledges for support of Diocese and National church are made.

Among the constructive efforts of the American church to better conditions among retired clergy was the institution of the Church Pension Fund. To inaugurate this, a campaign for $12,000,000 was conducted in 1916. Trinity parish was alloted $2,500 as its portion of this. When the campaign was over, Trinity parish had pledged $3,700.

In 1916 the Diocesan Council was held at Trinity. The Rector reported 612 communicants, 968 baptized members.

Choir and Music

Since under Dr. Evans' leadership there took place marked development and improvement in the music of the parish, it is well to place here a brief sketch of that department of Trinity church.

The first pipe organ was placed in the church 80 or 90 years ago, shortly after the erection of the present building. According to available records it was used for something like 40 to 50 years. This organ was in the "choir loft," or western gallery. Here, under the direction of Prof. Louis Platé, probably the first paid organist of the parish, and others who followed, a volunteer choir rendered the church music.

In 1894 a "fine new organ" was installed in the south transept. This was a Jardine organ, costing about $3,500, and true and sweet of tone until it wore out. It was in use for nearly forty years. Changes were made in the chancel at this time too, to accommodate choir stalls there; a choir-room was added back of the south transept, and a vested choir introduced.

Removal of the choir and organ from the loft left that space for sittings for the congregation. Almost at once it became the favorite of students of the South Carolina college and other young men and boys. The generations who have sat here can be traced by the carved names and initials of many past and present members of the parish. Some of the letters are dimmed with years, others done as lately as the warm spring Sundays of 1937 are white and new.

With the vesting of the choir and the addition of boys to that group, came a new avenue of service for women; namely care of vestments and supervision of the boys. Among those whose devoted service in this field won them the name of "choir mothers," and sent scores of mischievous lads into the choir stalls looking like newly fledged cherubs, have been Mrs. Clark Waring, Mrs. Anna Legare, Mrs. John Bollin, Mrs. J. L. Denny, Miss Carrie Berry, Mrs. E. C. McGregor, Mrs. J. G. Prioleau and others.

The organ bought in 1894 began to develop serious defects in its latter years. What tempermental organists may have whispered to it to keep it going, or thought of it when it occasionally broke down completely in the midst of service, is part of the unwritten history of the musical development of the parish.

Finally, after the need had become imperative, a new organ was purchased in 1933. This was in the depths of the black depression of 1929-34. The undertaking was a courageous one. The cost was $12,000, a price far below the value of the instrument. Installation necessitated building changes that cost about $2,700.

It was through the wish of the Rector, Dr. Henry D. Phillips that the church be appropriately and beautifully furnished for the honor and worship of God and the uplifting of the congregation, and due to the special interest of himself and one other of the music lovers of the parish that this exceptional opportunity to secure a fine organ was taken advantage of.

Morris C. Lumpkin sometime member of the vestry and of the choir, had an intense desire to see Trinity church have this organ. As said above, economic conditions were bad in the extreme and many members of the congregation were fearful of taking on additional obligations at this time. Mr. Lumpkin, however, gave assurance of his generous support, and by his enthusiasm for the proposal swept the congregation, with him into a spirit of determination to carry through this needed improvement for the church. At a special meeting of the congregation it was unanimously voted to purchase the organ. Groups, organizations and individuals joined heartily in the movement, defied lowered income and shaken morale, to work for the organ fund.

Funds came in from the estates of Mrs. Malvina B. Waring and Mrs. Louisa C. Shand. The Woman's Exchange Chapter of the Daughters of the Holy Cross made a substantial donation. Musicales, educational moving pictures, and a variety of other entertainments turned a few dollars here and there for payments on the organ.

At the death of Mr. Lumpkin there was still a large sum due on the organ. Mrs. Lumpkin asked the privilege of completing the payment in full in memory of the persistent and earnest desire of her husband that Trinity should have an organ that comported with the dignity of the parish services.

The regularly employed organists at Trinity church for the past 60 years approximately, so far as can be learned, have been: Prof. Louis Platé, Miss Bartlett, Daniel H. Wilson, Prof. George P. McCoy, Mr. Pearson, Mr. Lovell, J. D. Smithdeal, Henry F. Anderson, Paul deLaunay, Mrs. Louise C. Summer, M. Berry Seay and Kenneth W. Baldwin.

Some of the others who have served temporarily were: Carlton W. Sawyer, Mrs. Joseph M. Bell, whose long service in playing at Lenten services and for Church school and meetings of various organizations puts her almost in the class of "regular" organists, Mrs. J. W. Haltiwanger and Mr. Church.

Some of the important voices in the choir have been: Mrs. Kate Sawyer Stark, Mrs. Anna M. Percival, Albert E. Fugle, Mrs. W. McB. Sloan, Mrs. Julia B. Heath, Mrs. John I. Sutphen, Mrs. Wm. F. Furtick, Mrs. Christie Benet, Mrs. Carl Summer, Mrs. W. O. Sweeney, Mrs. A. S. Salley, David B. King, Robert E. Lafaye, John G. Prioleau, Morris C. Lumpkin, E. T. Cato, and many others.

There have been families of whom every member, certainly every child, has sung in the Trinity choir at one time or another.

Most of the singers listed above served for many years. Mrs. Furtick's sweet soprano has been enjoyed by our congregation for about 32 years. Her 25th anniversary as a member of the choir was celebrated about 1929 with a surprise party for her, at which she was presented with a substantial token of the sincere gratitude and friendship of the congregation.

Many persons remember gratefully her gracious and voluntary contributions to the music at funeral services and interments. Hundreds of times her sweet voice has softened the sorrows of those sad occasions.

In 1909 is found the first record of regular salaries for singers in the choir, though before that individuals had received gifts in appreciation of their services. The boys of the choir, however, were paid very small sums for their service from the time the boys' voices were introduced.

The choir today is made up of a group of paid singers, the leading voices these, and a large number of volunteer singers, boys, girls and adults.

III

WORLD WAR PERIOD

1917-1922

The year 1917 saw America enter the World War. As in the War between the States, the congregation of Trinity went all the way with the cause in which it believed. Almost 120 of its young men, and a few young women, were enlisted in army, navy, marine corps, and in the authorized welfare agencies with the armed forces. Three made the supreme sacrifice; one sleeps in Trinity churchyard, and two rest in France.

The Rev. Mr. Finlay obtained a year's leave of absence from the parish to go to France as a Y. M. C. A. worker with the A. E. F.

There was scarcely a member of the parish who did not do some war work. With the coming of Camp Jackson to Columbia soldiers by thousands were in the city at almost all times. For these the church did what it could by way of entertainment. Receptions, in the parish house, Sunday dinners in the parish house, Saturday night parties, also in the parish house, were carried on for many months while Camp Jackson was an important army base. As many as 150 to 200 soldiers were often at the Saturday evening entertainments. Young women and girls of the parish helped with the entertaining and older women chaperoned. At Sunday dinners for soldiers there were often from 75 to 100 guests. A special evening service with informal reception afterwards was held for many months during 1917-1919. After the Armistice, while there were still many patients at the base hospital at Camp Jackson, a motor corps of members of the parish and the Red Cross brought convalescents in for services, many of these men who were making their first efforts at rehabilitation following their wounds of body and spirit overseas.

It is not too much to say that many thousands of soldiers at Camp Jackson were reached by Trinity parish in its extensive efforts in their behalf. During these war years and immediately following, a substantial sum was carried in the budget for "Soldier Entertainment," this supplemented of course by individual contributions of money as well as service.

The parish was named as one of the authorized units of the vast "Community Club" which served soldiers throughout the nation.[19]

During the absence of the Rector in France in 1918-1919, the parish was served for several months each by the Rev. Edmond Bennett, D. D.; the Rev. Robb White, then a chaplain in the army and stationed at Camp Jackson; the Rev. G. Croft Williams, the Rev. H. M. Dumbell, and the Rev. E. A. Penick, Jr.

The Rev. Mr. Finlay was welcomed home in the summer of 1919. Immediately the parish entered upon the intense activity of the Nation-Wide Campaign, the plan of the National Church for enlisting every parish and mission and every individual of the Church in the service of God and man.

The parish was enthusiastic in its support of this movement, and was intimately associated with it; for Diocesan offices of the N. W. C., as it was generally called, were opened in the parish house at this time. Later, upon organization of the Executive Council of the Diocese, headquarters were maintained in the parish house until the old Satterlee Hall was torn down to make way for the new.

Trinity was well represented in the Nation-Wide Campaign, with Hon. R. I. Manning and Carroll H. Jones and the Rector on the first Diocesan committee.

On October 12, 1920, a special convention of the Diocese was held in Trinity church for the purpose of electing a Bishop-Coadjutor. The Rev. K. G. Finlay was elected. His rectorship

---

[19]A good account of war work of parish is found in report of Vestry to congregational meeting Easter Monday, 1919.

terminated December 31, 1920; but he assisted in the affairs of
the parish until his successor took charge.

The consecration of Bishop Finlay, in Trinity church, January 20, 1921, with Rt. Rev. Wm. Alexander Guerry, D. D., as consecrator, was not only a ceremony of unusual beauty and dignity attended by a gathering of distinguished Bishops, clergy and laymen and many friends of other communions, but it was the occasion for the parish to unite in showing to their Rector, now leaving them for a larger field, their warm affection and loyalty. He was presented by the parish with his episcopal robes, and by the Daughters of the Holy Cross with a pectoral cross. To him and Mrs. Finlay was given, at the luncheon following the consecration, a silver service.

IV

THE PARISH TODAY

1922——

On January 1st, 1922, the Rev. Henry D. Phillips assumed the rectorship of Trinity parish, he and his family moving into the rectory at 909 Sumter street, which had been recently purchased by the parish.

Under Dr. Phillips' leadership the parish has almost doubled in membership (1922, communicants 751; 1937, communicants 1,200).

The handsome and well planned parish house, dream of the congregation for more than a generation, became a reality in 1925-26. A new organ was installed in 1933. The church has been re-decorated within, the pews recovered, kneelers installed, and appropriate lighting provided. Several memorial windows have been placed, a new heating plant put in, and many other improvements and additions made to the fabric of the church.

There is not a member of the congregation, looking with full appreciation upon these added "things", who does not feel that these are but contributory to Dr. Phillips' higher aim of spiritual growth of the individual members, and greater usefulness of the parish to community, Diocese, nation and world.

Dr. Phillips, with a genuine gift for planning, has coordinated the work of the men and of the women of the parish so as to allow of great breadth in scope of activities without sacrifice

REV. H. STRINGFELLOW
Assistant Rector, 1874-1878

of the efficiency of the smaller groups these organizations once
were.

The Church school, under his direction has been brought
to a high state of usefulness.   Well-staffed, with a regularly
employed director of religious education, and with a curriculum approved by national authorities in religious and Church
training, the school is carrying on effectively the work of building for the parish-to-be.

The business administration of the parish under the present
Rector's clear-seeing plans is as orderly and systematic as that
of any corporation in secular business.   His commonsense and
sane judgment, shown in his parish affairs, have made him a
valuable addition to Diocesan and national councils.

Though parish duties are heavy, Dr. Phillips arranges, with
the distinct approval and pride of his congregation, to give of
his time and talents to community enterprises also.   He is a
leader in civic work, particularly in the annual community chest
campaigns and in the year-round managements of the community
chest funds.

Perhaps after all, however, Dr. Phillips' greatest gift is a
pastoral one.   He has rare ability in reaching and touching in
informal, intimate, even tender, relations the lives of members
of his congregation.

In 1923, after consideration over a period of about 15 years
the Diocese of South Carolina was divided, the new Diocese
of Upper South Carolina being erected, with the Rt. Rev. K. G.
Finlay, Coadjutor of the old Diocese, Bishop of the new Diocese.
Trinity parish had an important part in the creation of the new
Diocese and has exercised wide influence in its affairs since.
To the $50,000 endowment fund raised for the new episcopate,
the parish contributed some $11,500, raised in a special cam-
paign under the chairmanship of David G. Ellison.

The Primary Convention of the new Diocese met in the parish
which provided its first Bishop.   This meeting was held October 10, 1922.

As the largest parish in the new Diocese, Trinity has made
important contributions financially and otherwise.   Headquarters are furnished in the parish house for the Bishop and the
Diocesan office.   In these offices and in other rooms in the parish
house are held many of the gatherings of Diocesan committees,

of the Executive Council, and of Diocesan committes of Woman's Auxiliary and of the Young People's organizations.

The Rector of the parish, Dr. Phillips, has served almost continuously since the founding of the Diocese as a member of the Standing Committee, and on the Executive Council as member of Finance and Field Departments and as chairman of both; also as trustee of the Voorhees Normal and Industrial school, as Trustee of Sewanee, and in other positions.

The late Hon. R. I. Manning was a member of the Executive Council from its organization, and from that time until his death, chairman of the Finance Department.

The late W. Anderson Clarkson was treasurer of the Diocese. J. Nelson Frierson has been the careful and efficient secretary of the Standing Committee for many years.

One of the first two women to serve on the Executive Council of the Diocese was Mrs. D. G. Ellison. Other women of the parish in this group at one time or another have been Mrs. James R. Cain and Mrs. Beverley Sloan, Mrs. Sloan serving now as a member. Mrs. Cain, too, was for a long period secretary of the Board of Trustees of Voorhees school.

Numbers of others have served on the Council.

Headquarters secretary of the Diocese from 1923 to 1926 was Mrs. William P. Cornell; succeeding her and serving from 1926 to 1936 was Mrs. Henry L. Forbes, both members of this parish.

Dr. Phillips has also won recognition in National Church affairs. He was one of the Committee of Seventy of some years ago, and has been a member of the National Field Department. He has been often elected deputy from this Diocese to the General Convention.

Hon. R. I. Manning was a member of the National Council for several years, his service terminating at his death in 1931. Mrs. James R. Cain was one of the first four women elected a member of the National Council. She holds this position now.

The Diocesan Convention met again in Trinity, in the new parish house, in 1928; and the Synod of the Fourth Province met here in the fall of 1929.

In 1928 the parish suffered a severe loss in the death of Miss Jennie G. Gibbes, for more than 30 years treasurer of the parish, and a devoted communicant of the parish. Before "Miss Jennie" became treasurer this office was filled usually by a member of the vestry. Available records show that treasurers have been C. J. Iredell, W. G. Childs, T. Hasell Gibbes. Following Miss Gibbes' death, Mrs. Charlotte M. Hutchison was made treasurer, and holds this position at present.

In 1916, Mr. Finlay was given an appropriation for a part-time secretary to help him with the many details of office work. His first secretary was Joseph McCabe. Others, some volunteer, some paid, helped Mr. Finlay for brief periods after Mr. McCabe left to enter the army in 1917. Upon the Rector's return from his war service in 1919, Mrs. Henry L. Forbes became his secretary. Mrs. Forbes was also Dr. Phillips' secretary from 1922 to 1926. Others in order of succession who have worked in the Rector's office have been Mrs. S. A. Irby, Mrs. E. C. Cathcart, Mrs. W. B. Wells, Miss Ella Parr Phillips, Mrs. Wells again, and since 1934, Miss Roberta Aldrich.

With all of America the parish and its members suffered in the depressed conditions of 1929-34. Contributions were smaller, bank failures swallowed some of the parish funds and much of the means of its members. Meanwhile, of course, calls for help increased.

When the canvass of 1933 showed a wide gap between pledges and budget, in spite of salary reductions and cuts in expenses wherever possible, the outlook was gloomy. At the beginning of the year the Rector bravely took the situation in hand, gathered the congregation and told them frankly how matters stood. Presented with a picture of the parish work and the Church's mission crippled by lack of funds, the congregation made a gift of sacrifice to supplement pledges, sufficient to carry the work along and to institute the much needed director of religious education.

Of both sentimental and practical interest is it to note that of the families known to have been active in the founding and early building of this parish, there are several which have been almost continuously represented in the membership, the counsels and the activities of the parish. Long service by individuals and by families has come to be a cherished tradition of the parish.

Added to these families who pioneered in the church's development, have been others who moved in later and who have rendered no less devoted service.

Some of those who have been members of this parish and have gone into the ministry of the Church have been the Rev. Sanders Richardson Guignard, the Rev. Hope Henry Lumpkin, Clark Waring,[20] the Rt. Rev. Albert S. Thomas, the Rev. Harold Thomas, the Rev. S. Thorne Sparkman, the Rev. William Wallace Lumpkin, and Allen Boykin Clarkson.[21]

Today, with the rapid growth of the city, there are scores of welcome new-comers in the parish. Old and new alike work shoulder to shoulder, moving forward together.

In the year 1937, the 125th anniversary of the founding of the parish, the congregation recovered in large measure from economic depression, has 1,200 communicants, 400 unconfirmed members. It is larger, stronger than ever before. It stands as one of the strong influences for good in the community and the state. It is a pillar of strength to the Diocese, and it is above all a busy, happy, united group of Churchmen working for the betterment of mankind and the glory of God.

---

[20]Died before his theological studies were completed.
[21]Now in Theological Department, University of the South.

REV. H. O. JUDD
Assistant Rector, 1878-1886
Rector, 1886-1887

CHURCH SCHOOL

In the realization that the Church school is the Church of the future, as well as the training ground for Christian character, this department of the parish assumes a place of importance second to no other enterprise of the Church. No story of Trinity parish is complete without the story of the Church school.

Early records of the Church school, known until the past ten years or so as the Sunday school, shared the fate of other parochial records; but it is reasonable to assume that when the handful of Episcopalians gathered together to establish a congregation of the Church in Columbia, these Churchmen, pioneers in the new capital of the state, saw to it that their children received instruction in the faith and practice of the Church. There is no way of knowing, however, when a Sunday school was formally established in the little mission in Columbia.

Annual report of Trinity church to the Diocesan Convention of 1836 shows that there was then an organized school here, of six teachers and about 35 white scholars. Practically the same numbers were reported from 1841-42-43. From the Rector's report in 1842 comes the statement that 30 to 40 children were "catechised", the last Sunday in each month.

By 1845 there is noted some growth, ten teachers, 35 white scholars and 40 Negro scholars. On through the Confederate war, in accordance with the practice of that day in the South, Negroes, slaves and their children, were part of the parish.

In 1856, the school had seven teachers and 40 to 50 white scholars; 40 children catechised each month. Subjects of instruction in the school were: "Beavan's Catechism, Questions on Collects, Questions on Gospels and Acts, Easy Questions on Watts' Hymns."[22]

There was a parochial school in operation at this time, supported by private subscriptions.

In 1860 there had been added to the subjects mentioned above "Trapier's, Glenn's and Calvary Catechism, taught by nine teachers to 78 pupils.

In 1863-64, the Sunday school had a staff of six teachers and from 20 to 50 pupils, all white. This great variation in student-body being no doubt due to the unsettled conditions prevailing at that time.

---

[22]Report of Dr. Shand to Diocesan Council, 1856, Journal of Diocese of South Carolina.

There was a small Sunday school building in the northeast corner of the church lot. This building was destroyed when the city was burned in 1865.

With the demoralization and dire poverty that enveloped the city at that time, there was small hope of a new building for many years. However, the members of Trinity parish did not lose their interest in religious education, and on Sundays gathered the boys and girls in the church building for instruction.

Struggling with poor equipment, the Sunday school went on. In 1869, the Rector included in his report to the Diocesan Council the statement that: "The destruction of the Sunday school building in the fire of 1865 has caused great inconvenience and interfered with increase of scholars and progress of the school." There were at this time only five teachers and 15 to 30 pupils.

However, by 1875 the school had grown to 146 pupils with 14 teachers.

By 1883 a definite movement was begun to erect a Sunday school building. Completed in 1886, it housed the school of that day amply. An Easter program of 1889 shows an enrollment of 111 students, 12 teachers, not including the Rector, Rev. Ellison Capers, who taught the Bible class of 37.

"Completely equipped," say the vestry minutes reporting acceptance of the new building from the Ladies Sunday School Committee in 1886; but the equipment, as some communicants of today still recall it, was indeed simple.

A low platform, curtained off at the eastern end, of the building, held the "infant class", which under the long and devoted service of Miss Eliza A. Carroll ("Miss Lilla") consisted of children from toddlers' size up to ten years of age or more. This warm-hearted teacher could not bear to part with her charges, and only as the platform became so crowded that some children had to sit on the outside steps, did she consent to promote a few of her long-legged boys and girls to higher classes.

Beyond the platform was the main hall. Benches of slatted oak were placed facing each other to accommodate class groups. Here were ten to 12 classes of six to ten pupils each. There was no regular promotion, a teacher keeping one class for many years.

Still preeminent in the curriculum were the Church catechism and the collects. Still in use for beginners was the "Cavalry" catechism. Classes were still "catechised." The effect of eight

or ten classes all in one hall reciting different sections of the catechism or the collect for the day was much like descriptions of
old-fashioned Chinese class-rooms.

There was a small library of distinctly "Sunday-Schoolish"
books; Maria Edgeworth and Miss Charlotte Yongue having
important place on the shelves.

Prominent in the furnishings of this old building was the
organ of chapel or cottage type. Somewhat wheezy at times,
but it set the tone and guided the voices of children in the spirited
strains of "Onward Christian Soldiers," and softly intimate lines
of "Jesus, Tender Shepherd," even as the more sprightly piano
accompaniments do today.

Lacking minutes and roll books, records of the Sunday school
and its staff are necessarily very inadequate. Names of some who
served as officers or teachers have been lost. Others are recalled
by older members of the congregation.

When the little Sunday school on Senate street was occupied in
1886, Captain C. J. Iredell was superintendent. His staff and
corps of teachers as published in 1889 is as follows: Librarian,
Mrs. C. W. Ravenel; teachers: Mrs. S. C. Goodwyn, Mrs. Porcher,
Miss Ellen Elmore, Miss Jane Reynolds, Mrs. Swaffield, Misses
Lilla and Sophie Carroll, Miss Thomas, Mrs. Bartlett, Miss
Capers and Miss Ruth Bartlett.

Dr. Evans served as superintendent of the school during part
of his rectorate, as did also Mr. Satterlee. Among those who
were superintendents after Captain Iredell were Wade Hampton Manning, William C. Swaffield, Judge A. C. Haskell.

Among teachers serving with these superintendents, some of
them under Capt. Iredell also, were: Miss Colie Goodwyn, who
taught for thirty years or more; Miss Rebecca Shand, who taught
continually until the death of her father, the Rev. Peter J.
Shand, and also taught in the Parochial school and in the Industrial school; Mrs. Ellison Capers, who had a class until
Bishop Capers' health failed; Mrs. Walter Taylor, H. P. Green,
Miss Caroline Heyward, Miss Lou Dwight (Mrs. E. C. Cathcart), Miss Marietta Cathcart (Mrs. Washington Clark), R. W.
Shand; Mrs. Allen Jones, to whose honor goes not only her own
long service, but the credit for having secured Miss Louly Shand
as a teacher, and Mrs. Albert R. Heyward.

In 1894 there were 182 pupils and 34 teachers.

Poor though the children of Trinity Sunday school were at
this time, with the post-war poverty of their section, the custom of having a Christmas tree for them was never established.
A tree for others less fortunate than themselves, for the children of the Industrial school, was provided some years; later
Trinity children sent gifts for children at Trinity mission, and
still later took up the annual custom of sending stockings and
gifts to children of the Church Home orphanage at the Christmas season.

Trinity Sunday school, however, was strong for the annual
picnic, given for many years in early summer. To children of
that day, whose recreation was often scantily provided for, these
occasions were rare treats. The pupils met in early morning at
the Sunday school, clambered or scrambled into big wagons
drawn by mules, ranged themselves on hard board seats, and
sang and shouted the whole of the way to the picnic grounds,
at "Millwood" or elsewhere beyond the city. Luncheon was
carried in unimaginable abundance, lemonade added by the
ladies of the parish. A day of games, wading and swimming,
and a joyous ride home, made an event which children of that
time regarded as but little less delightful than Christmas itself.
So important in the child life of that time was the Sunday school
picnic, that every child in the public schools was allowed to
miss one day in spring to attend the picnic of his particular
Sunday school.

The Sunday school picnic passed with the fading of the horse-
and-buggy age; when a trip to a pond or a club became almost a
daily summer amusement to most of the members of the school,
the organized picnic was no longer necessary nor desired. But
the annual Trinity picnic, and the little wooden Sunday school
building are fondly entwined in the memories of those who knew
both.

The Church catechism and the stately prose of the collects
held their place in the Sunday school; but there were introduced toward the end of the century graded lesson books. Later
the Rev. Mr. Satterlee instituted a system of lessons on the Bible
requiring written answers.

In connection with the Sunday school, the Rev. Mr. Satterlee organized a group of smaller boys of the parish into a club
known as the "Boys of Trinity." The devoted service of Mrs.

T. K. Legare, Sr., Miss Carrie Berry and other women of the parish in connection with this club is recalled. This group was a forerunner of the Boy Scout troop of nearly a generation later, sponsored by the Men's Club and under the leadership of the Rev. Mr. Finlay.

As the parish grew, the Sunday school grew and crowded the small building. Agitation for a new building increased and came to fruition in 1907 with the erection of one section of the planned building. Built in a fashion considered very desirable then, that of a central hall with class rooms cut off by folding partitions, this parish house was soon outgrown and outmoded.

Now the school must meet in two sections. For a time the senior group met in the morning and the younger children in the afternoon. Then all met at the same hour, but all except the primary department were housed in the church.

Under the rectorate of the Rev. Mr. Finlay, James A. Cathcart was for eleven years superintendent of the junior department. Before that O. Frank Hart had been superintendent of the whole school. Mr. Hart was active in urging a new building, better equipment and better trained teachers. When at the Rector's request he became superintendent of St. Timothy's Sunday school, James S. Middleton became superintendent at Trinity.

Carroll H. Jones, beginning his term under the Rev. Mr. Finlay, was superintendent for 18 years. James H. Fowles was superintendent of the senior department for several years and James B. Murphy of the junior department. Robert Moorman served as superintendent of the intermediate department.

Miss Mary Heyward (Mrs. William Babcock) was secretary of the primary department for many years. F. G. Swaffield, too, served as secretary in the Church school.

Young people's work took on new impetus under the leadership of Rev. Mr. Finlay. Besides the Boy Scout troop already referred to, there was organized a group of Trinity boys and girls in a unit of the Christian Endeavor society, there being at that time no organization of the Church for boys and girls together. This unit lasted for several years and trained a group of the youth of the parish in breadth of view and strong ideals of social obligation, influence of which is felt in the congregation yet.

In curriculum, in enlarged missionary outlook and in teacher-training, the Church school made marked strides. The Lenten offerings, for general missions, increased. The Christian Nurture series of Church school material was introduced. Teachers were sent to the summer training school at Sewanee, and the Rector conducted, more than one winter, a special Bible class for Church school teachers, and a mid-week Bible class for women of the parish.

Toward the latter part of Dr. Finlay's rectorate he gathered together a group of Church students in attendance at the University of South Carolina and organized the College Men's Bible class. Dr. Phillips with his unusual gift for making close contact with and influencing young men, has carried the usefulness of this class to a high degree. The group, meeting once a week during the college term, for supper in the parish house and Bible study and discussion afterwards, has both social and religious aims, and is held to be one of the constructive Christian influences of campus life. From members of this class a number have entered the ministry, 13 of them since 1922.

With the long-desired new parish house, completed and occupied January 1926, all activities for young people showed marked expansion. A lay assistant to the Rector was employed. John Adger Manning being the first of a series of young men so engaged. In this capacity following Mr. Manning were John M. Bell, John Ellis Craps, Archibald Hardy, Jr., Allen Clarkson and Williams McIver Bryan.

Under these young men, church work for boys in particular was strengthened. The Junior Brotherhood of St. Andrew for several years was a force in Church training. The Boy Scout troop No. 14 became one of the leading troops of the city.

The Young People's Service League, including under its national organization both boys and girls, too, was able to function with more effectiveness when suitable place for meetings, for mid-week activities and for recreation were provided in the new parish house.

The parish house, however, was designed primarily to meet the need of fitting accommodations for the Church school. Under the favorable physical conditions here provided the school has grown in numbers, but more noticeably in the quality of work done in the school.

Not to the parish house alone, however, can be attributed the progress of the Church school. To the far-seeing planning of the Rector, to the steadily increasing efficiency of teachers and officers, and to the employment of a director of religious education can be laid most of the success of the school. In 1934 Miss Roberta Aldrich became secretary to the Rector and director of religious education in the parish.

The Church school today is organized along approved educational principles in religious and spiritual training. The Christian Nurture series is still the principal text. The school works in the Five Fields of service. For the parish they provide the Junior choir, servers at communion services, and the girls who serve at suppers.

The Young People's service held every Monday during Lent, culminating with the service on the afternoon of Easter, when the Church school offering is presented, has come to be among the vital features of parish life, not only for the young people themselves, but for many adults.

The Cradle Roll or Little Helpers, which enrolls babies under three years of age, is doing valuable work in giving children their first contact with the Church school. A service with a pretty cradle-rocking ceremony is held for this group twice a year.

There is today a staff of 52 men and women, who besides giving Sunday after Sunday their services in the class-room, attend faithfully the monthly teachers' meetings, when problems and plans of the school are discussed. Of today's staff there are seven whose service with the Church school covers a period of twenty years or more. These are Mrs. Jos. M. Bell, James R. Cain, Mrs. T. M. DuBose, Jr., Mrs. H. Bland Hammond, Miss Louly Shand, Miss Mamie Shand and Dr. N. B. Heyward.

Some of the staff attend each summer the Adult Conference at Kanuga; and a number of the Church school pupils and young people attend the Young People's Conference and Junior camp held at this large training center whose establishment, growth and success are largely the fruits of the efforts of a former Rector of the parish, the Rt. Rev. K. G. Finlay.

For the last three years Trinity Church school has won first place among exhibitors at the Kanuga Adult conference.

The enrollment for the year 1936-37 in the Church school was 340 pupils, with an additional membership of about 45 in the College Men's Bible class. Surveys of the families in Trinity show that the percentage of children of suitable age enrolled in the Church school is high. Interest and coöperation of parents generally is excellent.

The school meets at ten o'clock overy Sunday morning. For nine months, following rather closely the schedule of the public schools, the regular session goes on. During the summer the organization is changed to meet the conditions arising from absence of many families from the city for part or all of the summer. A special course is given for summer work, and efforts are made to sustain interest by a variety of methods. One of the most interesting of these is the plan of outdoor teaching, the course involving correlation of parts of the Bible story with the outdoor scene.

Superintendents of the several departments of the School at present are Geddings H. Crawford, Dr. N. B. Heyward and Miss Louly Shand.

PARISH HOUSE

TRINITY PARISH HOUSE

In any history of the parish house it is proper to give an account of the buildings used as a parish house or Sunday school building, prior to the erection of the present building.

John P. Thomas, Jr., who has probably been a member of Trinity church longer than any other living person, states that there was originally a small Sunday school building on the northeast corner of the church property, fronting on Gervais street and next to the Gray residence; that this building had semicircular seats which rose from a platform, and that it was destroyed by fire in 1865.[23] There is extant no picture of this building or any further description of it.

The next Sunday school building was on the site of the present building, a small wooden structure in which the Sunday school classes met. There were no class rooms, but the benches were arranged in the open hall so as to make separate spaces for the different classes. In the minutes of the congregational meeting of March 26, 1883, appears the following statement: "The question of the Sunday school building was brought up. The subject was discussed at some length."

Following this meeting a committee of the vestry was requested in April 1883, to make plans and receive bids for such a building. Nothing, however, seems to have been accomplished until, in February, 1885, a letter was presented to the vestry "from a number of ladies of the congregation interested in a Sunday school building." A resolution was adopted stating "that the ladies of Trinity church be hereby granted sufficient ground in the southeast corner of the lot south of the church upon which to erect a Sunday school building in accordance with their petition." To act with the Ladies Sunday School Committee, of which Miss Ellen Elmore was chairman, R. S. DesPortes, Clark Waring and John Taylor were appointed from the vestry.

Later mention is made of 'sums due the ladies," from the vestry for the building. Again, a committee was appointed to help the ladies collect $200 due their committee.

Finally, on November 1, 1886, the Ladies Sunday School Committee presented as their final report, the completed building, "furnished with seats, stoves, organ, book-cases, charts, etc."

---

[23]Report of Dr. Shand to Diocean Council, 1869.

So this second Sunday school building, which served for 40 years, was evidently largely the fruit of efforts of women of the congregation. Records of the women's organizations of that time are lost, and only these bare statements in the vestry's minutes hint at the toil and labor, the cake sales, the suppers and bazaars, that went into the erection of that small wooden chapel where many of the present leaders in parish life received their early Church training.

This building was used continuously until the erection of Satterlee Hall.

At the congregational meeting on April 24, 1905, the treasurer's report shows the collection of a fund in memory of Churchill Satterlee, the Rector, who had died shortly before that time, and who had really instituted the movement for the new parish house. Also a gift in memory of Allen Singleton Green; and the Easter offering which was applied to that purpose. At this meeting the building committee submitted a report which recommended that the drawing submitted by G. E. Shand as architect be adopted as the ultimate plan of the parish house to be erected in the southeastern section of Trinity churchyard. Further, that the work of building the main hall for Sunday school rooms be begun at once, and pushed as rapidly as the funds in hand would permit; and that thereafter the tower and other rooms in the proposed structure be built, as soon as funds were available therefor. It was further recommended that the whole building stand as a memorial to the dead of Trinity church, and be called Trinity Parish House, and that the Sunday school room be called "Satterlee Hall" in memory of Churchill Satterlee, who originated the movement. No action was taken on this recommendation.

On April 1, 1906, a meeting was held in the parish house, and the Building committee reported that it had selected G. E. Shand as architect, and plans had been prepared by Shand & Lafaye. That $1,000.00 had been given by Mrs. DesPortes and $3,000.00 additional pledged by various members of the congregation prior to the death of Mr. Satterlee. That only a small part of the pledges had been paid, and the subscribers generally declined to pay until work was begun, that the work could not be done with the funds in hand, and that the pledges would be lost if the work were not started. The Committee, therefore, had recommended that the work start and progress as far as funds would permit. This plan was approved by the vestry, but upon being submitted to the congregation no action had been taken. The Committee thereupon decided to proceed, and meantime the funds had been increased by the offering on All Saints' Day of 1904 and the Easter offering in 1905, nearly all of which latter amount was given by friends of Mr. Satterlee outside of the state in memory of him. Bids were called for, but none for less than $20,000.00 was received. It was then resolved to build as far as the funds in hand would permit and Hasell Thomas was employed to superintend the work. It was begun early in the summer of 1906. The Committee reported that the building so far had cost $6,028.40 and that the additions to complete the building as planned would probably add $14,000.00 to this figure.

The corner-stone of this building was laid on June 20, 1906. During the absence of the Rector, Rev. Charles Martin Niles, the Rt. Rev. Ellison Capers, D. D., Bishop of the Diocese of South Carolina and former Rector of Trinity church, officiated, assisted by Rev. Samuel Moran, who was in charge of Trinity mission. The address of the occasion was delivered by Hon. W. C. Benet, formerly a circuit judge of South Carolina, and at that time a member of the congregation.

The wardens of the Church at that time were Allen Jones and John T. Seibels and the vestrymen, Dr. T. M. DuBose, H. P. Green, G. A. Guignard, John Taylor, T. H. Gibbes, A. S. Gaillard and G. E. Shand. The treasurer of the Church was Miss Jennie G. Gibbes and the organist Henry F. Anderson. The contents of this box were as follows:

The Churchman and Living Church of June 16, 1906; The Diocese of May and June 1906; Trinity Evangel of March and April 1906; Spirit of Missions of May 1906; Journals of the Diocesan Conventions of 1904 and 1905; copy of the proceedings in celebration of the 50th Anniversary of the Rectorship of Rev. Peter J. Shand, D. D., Brief Outline of the History of Trinity Church with list of officers, Architects and Builders. Copy of *The State* of June 20, 1906; and a view of Columbia.

This parish house consisted of a fair-sized auditorium with a rostrum at the end of the auditorium, and with class rooms ranged around the sides, which could be cut off from the main auditorium by sliding partitions. It served the purpose of the congregation for many years; but as the congregation increased in number and the uses of the building multiplied, it became inadequate, and there arose a constant demand from the congregation for its completion. Finally, it was decided to devote the Easter offering of 1920 to this purpose, and notice was given that any persons desiring to create memorials could do so by designating their gifts at this time. A considerable sum of money was collected at this offering and ultimately used in the erection of the present building. A list of these and other memorials in the parish house will be found in the chapter on Memorials in this volume.

This agitation for completion of the building continued throughout the years until finally in 1924 it was decided definitely that something should be done. The matter was given careful consideration by the vestry, and by the congregation. It was then decided that it would be better to abandon the old building and build a new parish house on the old site. At that time Dr. Henry D. Phillips was the Rector of the church and it was under his able and enthusiastic leadership that the movement took definite form. It was decided that the first step in building a new parish house should be the payment of the indebtedness of the church, which amounted to approximately $4,000.00. Accordingly, a special meeting of the men of the congregation was held in Satterlee Hall in the early part of 1924, and at that time the situation was explained, and donations were requested for the purpose of paying the debt as a necessary preliminary to the building of a new parish house. The response was enthusiastic, practically the whole amount being pledged at that meeting, and thereupon plans were set in motion for a new parish house.

In 1922, the congregation had approved the purchase of a new rectory at 909 Sumter street, and the abandonment of the old rectory at the southeastern corner of Sumter and Senate streets, which had been used as a rectory since shortly after the destruction of the first rectory in 1865.

On March 3, 1924, the vestry approved the sale of the old rectory property to the State of South Carolina for $34,500.00 to be used by it for the erection of a State Office Building. Subsequently, on April 1, 1924, this sale was approved by the con-

REV. ELLISON CAPERS, D. D.
Rector, 1887-1893

gregation. The Rector was then authorized to appoint committees and confer with Hobart Upjohn, a church architect of New York, as to the proposed new parish house. On April 14, 1924, Mr. Upjohn was definitely employed as architect and was directed to employ a local associate. The estimated cost of the proposed building at that time was $90,600.00. At the same meeting the Parish House Finance committee, consisting of Christie Benet, chairman, Carroll H. Jones, vice-chairman, and W. Anderson Clarkson as secretary, with other active members of the congregation, was appointed.

An intensive campaign was instituted at once, and on May 8, 1924, a special meeting of the Men's Club was held in the parish house for the purpose of working out definite plans. At this meeting, which was presided over by Christie Benet, Chairman of the Finance committee, plans of the proposed building were explained, the general and special needs were discussed and the financial plans stated. All of the men present were pledged to attend church the following Sunday and to attend a luncheon at Satterlee Hall on Wednesday, May 14th, at which time the campaign for pledges would formally start. With an enthusiastic band of solicitors, a two-day campaign was put on which resulted finally in collecting cash and pledges of $76,465.15. This, with the accumulated parish house funds, and the proceeds from the sale of the rectory, was deemed sufficient to proceed with the new building.

Included in the amount given was $4,772.15 by the Daughters of the Holy Cross, a fund which they had been accumulating for this purpose since 1912; and $3,000.00 by the Woman's Exchange, an organization sponsored by the Daughters of the Holy Cross; all of which was in addition to $7,000.00 given by the Woman's Exchange in previous years. Surely the women did their full part.

As the canvass progressed through the afternoon, word spread, without any definite announcements, as to its success. Canvassers, passing each other on the steps of the parish house, or meeting a moment at the gate of the churchyard, communicated their good cheer to each other. Somehow the word went the rounds that the work was going well, and finally that pledges in hand were up to the needed amount to begin on the long-desired new parish house.

Then, quietly, again without any definite announcement, the Rector, canvassers and other members of the congregation repaired to the church for a service. With the sense that there was a great day's work behind them, and better days ahead for the work of the Church in this parish, the congregation offered genuine and heartfelt prayers of thanksgiving. This inspiring service was one of those rare occasions when worship truly sprang from the spirit of the worshippers.

A Parish House Building Fund committee was appointed consisting of A. McI. Griffin, chairman; John D. Bell, treasurer, and Wm. S. Nelson and H. J. Gregg of the Finance committee of the vestry, ex-officio; and a Building committee consisting of Rev. Henry D. Phillips as chairman, W. M. Shand, G. A. Guignard and A. McI. Griffin. Mr. Upjohn had named James B. Urquhart of Columbia as associate architect and the work of final preparation of the plans was undertaken. A Committee on Details and Plans, which included representatives from the various organizations of the parish, was appointed consisting of W. M. Shand as chairman, G. A. Guignard, W. M. Shannon, W. M. Manning, Carroll H. Jones, Robert Moorman, Miss Louly Shand and Mrs. Christie Benet.

The plans and specifications being finally approved, bids were opened on September 3, 1924, and at that time the lowest bidders were as follows:

J. C. Heslep, Columbia, General Contractor	$104,000.00
W. B. Guimarin Co., Columbia, Plumbing	6,581.78
B-C Electric Company, Columbia	4,150.00
	$114,731.78

With the cloister, which was not included in the above bid, and fees of the architect and incidental expenses, this would bring the total cost of the building to $128,548.92, which was more than was available. The vestry then authorized the construction of a building with cloister to cost $114,000.00, exclusive of fees. The plans were then revised so that finally the total cost of the building, including the cloister, was brought within this figure, and the estimated cost with all commissions to $121,571.00. The Finance committee reported that they had in hand and in pledges, less estimated interest charges and shrinkage of pledges, a total of $121,591.64, whereupon the Building committee was authorized to sign the contracts and the work was begun.

The cornerstone was laid on March 9, 1925, with appropriate exercises. In addition to the contents of the box in the cornerstone of the former parish house, there were placed in the cornerstone copies of that day's issue of the two daily papers, *The State* and *The Record;* proceedings of the Second Annual Convention of the Diocese of Upper South Carolina; Roster and Year Book for 1924 of the Women's Auxiliary, Upper South Carolina Branch; *Piedmont Churchman* of February 1925; Trinity Church Bulletin of March 8, 1925; "History and Traditions of Trinity Church, Columbia," by Robert Moorman, Esq.; a Parish House Pledge card; list of contributors and a list of the persons in whose memory contributions had been made; the names of the architect, builders and committees of the parish house, and miscellaneous views of Columbia.

The building progressed without unusual incident and was formally opened for use on January 14, 1926. On this occasion at a full gathering of the congregation the keys of the building were formally delivered to W. M. Shand of the Building committee by J. C. Heslep, the contractor. The keys to the Diocesan headquarters were delivered to Bishop Finlay by G. A. Guignard, the senior warden, and talks were made by Dr. Phillips, Mr. Upjohn and others.

The building has admirably fulfilled the purposes for which it was designed. The Rector has an office, in which the vestry meetings are also held; and the Bishop of the Diocese has his office in the Diocesan headquarters. The auditorium is used for an assembly-room for the Church school, for congregational meetings and for meetings of Daughters of the Holy Cross, Men's Club, and other organizations of the parish, and has proved ample for these purposes. There are separate class rooms for the Church school, some of which are large enough to take care of meetings of committees from the various organizations of the parish.

As part of the necessary equipment there was installed a modern kitchen, which is in constant use for the preparation of refreshments for meetings of the Men's club, Business Women's group, College Bible class and other meetings, and which has proved adequate for the service of such large gatherings as the parish supper. The gymnasium and basketball court in the basement, in addition to its constant use by the young people of the congregation, is used for other gatherings, so that the building is not only the center of the work of the Diocese and of the parish, but is a social and recreational center for the community as well.

The final cost of the building was $122,794.00. Unfortunately, the years of depression came before the pledges were all payable, and there was a larger shrinkage in the amount collected than had been reasonably anticipated. This fact also entailed additional payments of interest on the funds borrowed in anticipation of such pledges; and although the congregation had every reason to believe the parish house would be completed free from debt, there was finally a balance due, which has been secured by an obligation of the church.

The present generation of members of the congregation, who are in large measure responsible for the erection of this fine building, feel a justifiable pride in the achievement. They felt that as former generations had handed down to them a beautiful old church and surrounding grounds without burden, that their addition of the parish house was nothing more than was to be expected of them.

REV. W. E. EVANS, D. D.
Rector, 1893-1900

WOMEN'S WORK

The women of Trinity church ever since its organization have done their part in the work of the parish. There are no records of these early organizations of the Church-women but the story has been passed on to succeeding generations.

It is known that there was a Benevolent Society and a Ladies' Aid, later called Beneficial Society.

An industrial school was established by the women in Dr. Shand's pastorate and was carried on through Rev. Mr. Capers' time. There is a record of a Christmas tree given in 1895 for the Industrial school. This school taught sewing to poor women of the community, and many came for miles to attend. The garments made were sold, enabling these women to be self-supporting. It was this school which prompted Miss Lucy Green to leave to Trinity the fund known by her name. She had long been in charge of the work. The fund was left to assist women to earn their living. It is now used to help educate young women who in this way become self-supporting.

The women of Trinity, before and after the Confederate War, conducted a Parochial school for the poor children of the city unable to attend the "pay school." Thus these Church-women lent their aid in keeping alive education and culture in the devastated capital of South Carolina, as other gentlewomen of that time did throughout the desolate South.

THE WOMAN'S AUXILIARY TO THE BOARD OF MISSIONS

(From information furnished by MRS. JOHN T. SLOAN, former president.)

In May, 1885, during the last year of the pastorate of the Rev. Peter J. Shand, Miss Emery came to South Carolina for the purpose of organizing a branch of The Woman's Auxiliary in this Diocese. She first met with the women in Trinity Church, Columbia; but it was in Charleston, in Grace Church, May 1885, that the organization of the South Carolina Branch was effected. Its first president was Mrs. Robert Wilson of Charleston, a daughter of the Rev. Peter Shand. Miss Kate Hampton of Trinity Church, Columbia, was elected second vice-president.

Mrs. Albert R. (Sallie C.) Heyward was the second president of the Diocesan Branch. She served from 1906 to 1912.

Trinity Parish has given to the Diocesan Auxiliary three other presidents, Mrs. Wm. P. Cornell, Mrs. James R. Cain, and Mrs. R. Beverley Sloan. Many women have served from this parish as officers or chairmen in Diocesan organization.

This parish has the honor of having the first elected president of the Provincial Branch, Mrs. James R. Cain. She is also the first member at large elected to the National Board from the South, and one of the first four women elected to the National Council of the Church.

Immediately after the organization of the Diocesan Branch of the Woman's Auxiliary, Trinity Church formed a parish branch of which Mrs. A. R. Heyward (Sallie Coles Green) was elected president; Miss Elizabeth Carroll, secretary and Mrs. Robert W. Shand, treasurer. The treasurer's books show only a small membership, but their gifts to the mission field were remarkable considering scarcity of money in the South at that time.

Mrs. Heyward served as president for 22 years, and for part of that time she was president of the Diocesan Branch also. Hers was a long and faithful service.

Presidents following her were: Mrs. Tucker H. Fisher, 1917 to May 1919; Mrs. Henry L. Forbes, 1919 to June 1922; Mrs. Cornell (Wm. P.), 1922 to 1924; Mrs. John T. Sloan, Sr., was elected in June 1925. She served until the Woman's Auxiliary united with the Daughters of the Holy Cross and became Daughters of the Holy Cross Unit of the Woman's Auxiliary to the National Council.

The Auxiliary had been a vital force in the parish for 40 years in its work for missions, and in its merger with the Daughters of the Holy Cross carried with it the missionary spirit to enrich and broaden the already wide scope of the larger group. At the time of this union the Auxiliary numbered 95 members.

There was a Chapter B of the Woman's Auxiliary, but the records are not complete. It was formed during the Rev. Mr. Finlay's rectorship and lasted until 1914, according to the minutes; then united with Chapter A.

THE WOMAN'S GUILD OF TRINITY CHURCH

The Woman's Guild of Trinity Church was organized by Dr. William E. Evans in 1894 when he first came to Trinity Church. It was intended primarily for work connected with the Church but the older organizations, Benevolent and Beneficial societies, were included as Chapters in the Guild; the other Chapters being Chancel, Church and Churchyard.

At first the Chancel Chapter had the care of the Altar, but later on the Altar Chapter was added as a separate unit. The Guild began with 38 members. Except for the treasurer's book, the records of this Society have been lost, so names of officers cannot be given.

The Chancel Chapter did a splendid work. Mrs. Stricker Coles was the first chairman of this Chapter. The vested choir was begun at this time and all vestments were made by the Chapter's members. This was a big undertaking. The pulpit as it now stands was their gift to the Church.

The cleaning of the Church was superintended every week by the Church Chapter.

The Guild had a large part in organizing the Woman's Exchange; all officers were from the Guild. In 1918 the Woman's Guild which had served for 24 years disbanded and became members of the Daughters of the Holy Cross, which then assumed their work; the Churchyard and Chancel Chapters and Altar Guild became Chapters of the Daughters.

Mrs. T. M. DuBose was president at the time and Mrs. James H. Fowles, president of the Daughters.

DAUGHTERS OF THE HOLY CROSS

NOTE: The following sketch contains information and quotations from a history of the organization written by Mrs. Tucker H. Fisher (Mary Stoney) several years ago; and also information from the minutes.

On January 11, 1894, Dr. William E. Evans, Rector of Trinity Church, called a meeting of young unmarried women of the parish to form a chapter of Daughters of the King, a national Church organization. This society required certain pledges of its members, and at the second meeting it was voted not to join this society as the members were not willing to take these pledges. Thereupon Dr. Evans suggested a society, not nationally affiliated, with the name Daughters of The Holy Cross. He impressed upon these young women the responsibility of living up to such a name. This name has been very dear to the society since that time. The society bearing this beautiful and significant name was organized with the following officers elected by the group: President, Miss Mary Stoney; vice-president, Miss Amy Waring; treasurer, Miss Kitty Tennent.

This group of young women chose as their motto, "In Hoc Signo Vinces"; as their badge, a small Maltese cross in silver, with the letters "I. H. S." on the arms. Red was named as the society's color.

This society, aiming to afford opportunity for any young women who cared to do so, to join, set its dues at ten cents a month. It then formed chapters to work in several fields. The plan, then, was that a woman belonged to the whole group, but selected work according to her particular interest. The five chapters founded with the original organization were: Sunday School Chapter, Visiting Chapter, Flower Chapter, Mission Chapter, Charity Chapter. Miss Isabel Robertson volunteered to paint cards to be used by the Flower Chapter. Mrs. A. E. Legare (Isabel Robertson) makes them now, a long period of unbroken service.

The first obligation assumed by the society was paying the rent on a small building on Gates street for St. Thomas' Mission, just organized by Dr. Evans with the help of the men of Trinity.

The first gift to the Church was the Processional Cross for the vested choir just organized. The next work undertaken, the placing of two windows dividing the front vestibule from the body of the Church, was a Memorial.

A Re-table of Vermont marble was next bought for the Altar. Enlarging its scope in 1900, the society began educational work. Mrs. W. McB. Sloan was president at this time. A young girl was helped through Winthrop College. This was the beginning of a great work, and since that time many young women have been helped in securing their education.

Also at this time, under Mrs. Sloan's leadership the Daughters undertook definite charity work. Reports of the Charity Chapter always stirred the members to renewed efforts of personal service. Thanksgiving baskets were packed and sent to the poor

REV. CHURCHILL SATTERLEE, D. D.
Rector, 1900-1904

of the parish about this time. This custom has been followed with but few breaks since. Mrs. Sloan, second president served from 1895 to 1901—a gold star president.

Mrs. Christopher FitzSimons succeeded her. The society had grown much larger by this time and in order to foster the close personal relationship of the smaller group, at Mrs. FitzSimons' suggestion, it was decided to meet in groups during Lent. At these "circle" meetings a member would read from suitable and seasonable books while others sewed. This plan added to the Easter offering, increased interest in the society and strengthened the feeling of fellowship. This custom lasted for many years.

The *Trinity Evangel* was published in 1904 by the Daughters with Mrs. Mary Carroll Screven editor, the subscription price 25 cents a year. The Rev. Churchill Satterlee, Rector (1901-1904) had begun a mission in Olympia village, and his missionary spirit strongly influenced the Daughters. Members worked extensively in this field. A cooking-school was begun in the Mission House and carried on for several years by Miss Mamie Shand. Also a large sewing-school was established in which many women of the society and congregation took part. The minutes of the Daughters covering this period have been lost so only from memory can this story be told.

Miss Louly Shand, third president, was elected September 1904. At this time a limit of two-year term was set for the president, and also there was instituted the rule of having the vice-president serve with expectation of succeeding as president.

Purchase of the Choir Stalls was the outstanding accomplishment at this time. They were a memorial to Mr. Satterlee who had died in 1904. They cost $700.00. With only 100 members and in those hard times this was a great accomplishment. An annual bazaar, as a means of raising funds, was begun about this time, and for several years was an event socially and financially helpful.

For the next few years the many projects of the Daughters were carried on effectively by the next two presidents, Mrs. Gadsden E. Shand, who served one year, and Mrs. A. B. Knowlton, two years. A few figures from the treasurer's book are of interest:

May 1908 to May 1909	$460.81
From May Festival	20.20
	$481.03
Spent	406.33
	$73.70

Dues ten cents a month with about 100 members. The difference made up by work done, and special gifts.

When Mrs. Frank Tompkins (Mattie Aldrich) became president, September 1909, the Rev. Mr. Finlay asked for the organization of a Woman's Exchange. He explained the great need at this time of depression, for women to have some means of earning a part of their living expenses in the home. He wished a board elected from the Guild and the Daughters of the Holy Cross to have charge. This was not expected to be a money-making undertaking, but a help to the community. Both the Guild and Daughters agreed to undertake the work and organized an Executive Board as follows: Mrs. John J. Seibels, president; Mrs. Charles H. Cabaniss, vice-president; Mrs. Tazewell Talley, treasurer; Miss Caroline Swaffield, secretary; with eight other members of the board. The first three were from the Guild. The board was made up of members from both societies. The Exchange opened for business December 15, 1909, in two rooms in what is now the First National Bank Building. Supplying work to women among the congregation and in the community, it at once met a great need and was a blessing to many. Lunches were served and catering was done later. The first day's business amounted to $32.96. The first year $1,302.59. The largest business was done in 1920-21. The Exchange then had 375 members and a total business of $43,631.41.

Many members depended upon the Exchange for support during the period of the War, with husbands and sons in their country's service. The Rector's vision had been realized. The Exchange had become a factor in the life of the city.

In all civic affairs the Woman's Exchange did its part, subscribing to Booster Campaign, "Buy a Bale of Cotton," "Near East Relief" and other movements. To Trinity Church it donated $100.00 to equip the first Satterlee Hall with china. For the present parish house the Board of the Exchange turned over to the Finance Committee:

April 1920 for parish house $ 7,000.00
Interest on this $1,000.00
Contributed to the same fund 1924 $3,000.00
In 1930 donated to the organ fund $4,341.00

The Woman's Exchange continued its useful work until 1930. By that time other community activities made its work no longer necessary or possible to finance.

Mrs. John J. Seibels was president throughout its history and many members of the original board held office to the end. Mrs. Tazewell Talley, the first treasurer, served later and for many years as the efficient manager. Mrs. John T. Sloan, a member of the board at the founding, was secretary when the end came. Mrs. Kirkman G. Finlay, Miss Caroline Swaffield and Mrs. Carroll Jones were on the Board from beginning to end.

Perhaps the most constructive piece of work done by the Daughters of the Holy Cross was entered upon in 1909, when they began the work which developed into the Ridgewood Tuberculosis Camp.

In a desolate room in a then miserable Poor House, a young woman was found ill with tuberculosis; there because no one would take her in, and there was at that time no place in the state where she could be treated. At a meeting of the Daughters it was decided to begin the work of establishing a camp. During Lent of that year the circles or groups worked to make the money. Dr. Fred Williams, Dr. Heyward Gibbes and Dr. N. B. Heyward came in turn before these groups, told the story of the great need, aroused enthusiasm, touched the hearts, and made these women more determined to accomplish the task.

The first offering placed in the plate at Easter was $100.00. The society then numbered 50, and every dollar raised meant sacrifice. After two years the fund for this work amounted to $500.00. With this the first free clinic for tubercular cases was established in Columbia, marking the first step to establishing a camp, for in this way the need was demonstrated beyond argument and the public was aroused.

Mrs. Tucker H. Fisher, chairman of the Daughters' work thus far, was made chairman of the committee formed by the Associated Charities to carry on the work begun by the Daughters.

In 1914 Ridgewood Camp was a reality. The work and interest of the women of this society have continued on through the years to the present time. The permanent camp as it stands today has the Administration Building named for "The Daughters of the Holy Cross of Trinity Church" in recognition of the part they played in establishing the camp now valued at $67,-000.00 with 20 cottages and with many gifts from churches and individuals in the community.

It is not too much to say that Ridgewood Camp could not have survived and attained its present size and usefulness without the unfailing zeal, the untiring efforts of Mary Stoney Fisher. She has been a member of the board through all these years. Several years ago, Dr. T. C. Lucas paid a tribute before the Forum Club of Columbia from which a quotation follows: 'It is impossible to mention the anti-tuberculosis movement in this state or to refer to the establishment of Ridgewood Camp without pausing a moment to lift our hats in respect and admiration to a little band of women known as the Daughters of the Holy Cross of Trinity Church. These devoted women in the spirit of the Master, unmindful of creed or color, have wrought a great work." Like the City of the Bible this camp "hath foundations whose builder and maker is God."

During Mrs. Frank Tompkins' term as president beside the beginning of the Tuberculosis Camp, the parish paper, *Trinity Leaflet* was published by the women; the older publication, *The Trinity Evangel* having been discontinued for some years. Here a tribute may be paid to Mrs. Frank Tompkins as she is now one of three gold-star presidents of the Daughters. She died 1918, eight years after her term of office. One who knew her in her work for the Daughters said of her: "Mattie Tompkins was an efficient and faithful worker. She had untiring energy and absolute loyalty to her Church and to the community, which she served in many notable undertakings."

Mrs. Charles H. Barron served one part year as president and Mrs. Edmund Joyner was elected to succeed her. She stipulated that she was to serve only the unexpired term. Her willingness to take up the work with little notice was greatly appreciated. An effort was made to rally all members to her aid. The Bazaar, as always, brought all together in the society's common cause for good, and stirred the members to renewed activity.

Mrs. Tucker H. Fisher became president in 1913. As Mary Stoney she had been the first president. The Bazaar was still a part of the yearly program, but during her term it was decided to try a Rally Day, each one of the Daughters by sacrifice and work to make as much as possible and present it on that day. It is recalled that Dr. Evans was present and spoke to the Daughters at their first Rally Day. Before the next year Dr. Evans had passed away, and the day was named in his honor "Founder's Day." He had said on that day a year before: "Daughters of the Holy Cross, what a name to carry on our banner! What a name under which to labor for the poor and the stricken."

During Mrs. Fisher's term *Trinity Parish Leaflet* came out with a "Special Daughters of the Holy Cross Number," and in this is a report from every Chapter. A short statement from each one will give the scope of the women's work at this period.

Charity Chapter: Hettie I. Earl, Chairman. Acting with the Associated Charities; clothing and fuel supplied, positions secured, books to enable children to attend school, Christmas baskets for the poor of the parish.

Flower Chapter: Minnie B. Hammond, Chairman. Flowers to hospital ward and strangers, and to sick in the congregation. Twenty-four members.

Door of Hope Chapter: Mable O'N. Gaillard, Chairman. Served one dinner a week, Mrs. Christie Benet in charge. A class conducted in reading and sewing.

Rescue Orphanage Chapter: Supplied clothes and a special treat every week.

Visiting Chapter: Katharine B. Hutchinson, Chairman. Daily visits to the hospital, sewing for wards.

Church Home Orphanage: Lucy L. Boykin, Chairman. Twenty-seven members. Meet and sew. One box a month sent. Value about $15.00.

Periodical Chapter: Louly Shand, Chairman. Magazines sent to community and county. Also to Trinity Mission and to a mission. Two hundred magazines a month given out.

Woman's Exchange: Caroline Swaffield, Chairman. Supplied work to two hundred women. "This being a period of depression the Exchange is greatly needed."

A membership Chapter is listed with Mazie Meighan as Chairman. Report on Tuberculosis work is made by the Treasurer of the fund "as the whole society has charge of this work"—Julia Joyner, Treasurer. The Editor of the *Parish Leaflet* signed J. E. P., remarks: "I stand aghast at what has been accomplished by these women. I hope all others may be aroused to follow in their steps."

Mrs. Robert Moorman's term began September 1915. A protest was made against some of the films being shown and Mrs. Moorman was asked to present the matter to those in charge.

Help was given the Columbia Children's Clinic which was begun a short time before. Some volunteered for work.

A budget was made for the society for the first time.

Covering the cushions of the Church was being considered but the expense was so great "the committee suggested to the vestry to abandon cushions and make the pews more modern."

At this time, May 1917, the Daughters began plans for work with the soldiers soon to arrive at Camp Jackson.

Mrs. James H. Fowles began her term in 1917 in the midst of War work. The Daughters agreed to keep open house in Satterlee Hall every Wednesday night. Mrs. Christopher Fitz-Simons was in charge with a committee to help. All members were expected to take turns in chaperoning and helping. Games were played and refreshments served. All were asked to invite soldiers into their homes, especially after Sunday service.

The Guild now became a part of the Daughters, which added the Chancel Chapter, the Church Chapter, and Churchyard Chapter to the list of Chapters.

The membership was now 225, with the added Guild membership. The War, with Camp Jackson a great army base, added work to every Chapter, but all was cheerfully done with a wonderful spirit shown. The Daughters invested $200.00 in Liberty Bonds.

At a meeting in June 1918, Mrs. Frank Tompkins in well chosen words spoke of the Rev. Mr. Finlay's leaving for France for War work. The secretary was asked to write to Mr. Finlay approving this step he was taking. A farewell reception was given him by the Daughters and Mrs. Finlay was sent on to New York with him to see him on his way.

The Daughters during the Rector's absence "carried on" even better than before. A feeling of personal responsibility seemed to come to all.

Mrs. David Ellison was president in September 1919. The building of the parish house was again a matter of interest and a committee was appointed to act with the vestry.

The Nation-Wide Campaign was now the program of the Church and Mr. Finlay, just back from France, spoke of the necessity of the women's doing a big part to make it a success. A dinner was served by the Daughters, the supper Chapter in charge, for the canvassers in the Nation-Wide Campaign. Mrs. Eugene McGregor was chairman of the supper committee. This had become a very active chapter.

The Lenten offering at this time, April 1920, reached the surprising figure of $1,008.52, up to this time the largest we had received. This fund was equally divided between the anti-tuberculosis work and the building fund for the parish house.

Mrs. Wm. P. Cornell at the May meeting explained the purposes of the Church Service League, a national Church organization of which every parish was asked to form a branch. A plan had been worked out by Mrs. Tucker Fisher, Mrs. Cornell, Mrs. Ellison and the Rector, by which the Daughters would be a unit of the Church Service League with the Woman's Auxiliary reporting their work through the one society. In this way the five fields of service required would be reached. The Daughters now worked in three—church, community and Diocese and the Woman's Auxiliary would add nation and world. In this way all conditions would be fulfilled without forming another society. This plan was discussed for several meetings. The Daughters stood firm on not giving up the beloved name. The Diocesan Branch agreed to the name Daughters of the Holy Cross Unit of the Church Service League.

By this time Mrs. Hammond was president, Mrs. Ellison having ony served one year.

Dr. Jane Bruce Guignard addressed the women on vice conditions in Columbia. She gave a forceful presentation. All Church women in the city were considering this evil and were urged to take a definite stand. In December the Daughters presented Rev. Mr. Finlay, soon to be made Bishop, a gold cross modeled after the old badge of the Daughters. Mrs. Hammond in her lovely way presented it saying "it expressed our love and loyalty." Mr. Finlay in accepting said he considered the gift conferred upon him a life membership in the Daughters of the Holy Cross and he would wear it with thoughts of all this organization represented.

In October 1921, women of the parish were asked to vote on the question, "Do you agree with Resolution No. 46 of the Lambert Conference, namely, 'Women should be admitted to those councils of the Church to which Laymen are admitted, and on equal terms." They voted "Yes."

The Finlay Chapter

At the beginning of Lent, 1920, Mrs. John D. Bell gathered together a group of the young women of the parish for a study of the Church's Mission under the leadership of Mrs. J. R. Cain. So much interest was developed during the study that when the class ended the group asked that some organization be made to hold them together for work as an expression of that interest. For a year a tentative organization functioned without any special name, but with a very active program in missions, social service and study, the group growing from 20 to 35 members. At the end of that time realizing that their program coincided with that of the Woman's Auxiliary they decided to affiliate with that organization, calling themselves The Finlay Chapter in honor of the former Rector, at that time Bishop of the Diocese.

For eight years the Chapter carried on a fine program of work and study; Alice Gregg was their prayer partner and regular contributions were made to the Missions of the Church at home and abroad; in social service their work was confined largely to the Alms House and the State Industrial School for Girls, though from time to time they accepted assignments from the Associated Charities of the city and a family was "adopted" for each Christmas.

The good work of the Chapter is evidenced by the fact that many of the leaders in the parish life of today receive their training in it. One very delightful feature of the annual program was a tea given each year in honor of the Bishop at which time a gift was made to aid his work in the Diocese.

After the organization of the Training Chapter with objectives similar to their own, the Finlay Chapter disbanded and its

REV. CHARLES M. NILES, D. D.
Rector, 1904-1907

members were absorbed in the other Chapters of the Woman's Auxiliary in the parish; but the pleasant and beloved custom of the annual Bishop's Tea has been continued by the larger group.

The Women's Bible Class had been taught formerly by the Rector but, when Dr. Phillips assumed the rectorship, he organized a Sunday morning men's class which he taught for a number of years. The class grew to a representative group of 75 men. Feeling that he could not take care of the women's class and the college men's class he asked Mrs. Moultrie B. Hutchinson to be leader of the women's group. She began this work in the fall of 1922. As a leader she did a most excellent work and enlisted the interest of a large group of women which filled the Bible Class room each Wednesday afternoon. The response of the members was most enthusiastic. The class from time to time gave expression to their appreciation—once in the form of a silver vase and other times with tokens of appreciation and devotion to their leader. The courses taught consisted of the first five books of the Old Testament, the Prophets, the Life of Jesus, the Life of St. Paul, the Acts of the Apostles, and the Gospel according to St. Mark. This class continued until the spring of 1928.

It is a fact of interesting note in connection with this Bible class that for the years beginning with the fall of 1922 and through 1923, there were 350 adults in the parish studying regularly each week some course on the Bible. This interest in the Bible and the courses given did much in laying the ground work for the spiritual understanding and development of the parish.

A large gathering of the women of the congregation met in January 1922, to greet Dr. Phillips, the new Rector. Dr. and Mrs. Phillips were introduced and welcomed by Mrs. H. B. Hammond. Dr. Phillips responded in a delightful way.

In 1923, Dr. Phillips worked out a plan for reorganizing the Daughters of the Holy Cross in accordance with plans of the National Church for women's work. Under this plan chapters were grouped in the following departments: Church and Church Extension, Finance, Religious Education, Christian Social Service, Publicity.

The Chapters at that time were: Charity, Flower, Supper, Door of Hope, Tuberculosis, Church Home Orphanage, Churchyard, Chancel, Altar, Finlay Chapter, Service Chapter, Periodical, Woman's Exchange and Visiting.

Adopted in 1923, under leadership of Mrs. Hammond, retiring president, and Mrs. Christie Benet, incoming president, this plan gave new impetus to the women's work. It provided unity with wide scope and great flexibility. This line of organization was so favorably regarded outside the Diocese that a request came to have it presented and explained at the Woman's Auxiliary triennial convention in New Orleans, where the National Executive Board of the Auxiliary endorsed the idea.

In January 1923, Mrs. Benet extended greetings to more than 200 women present at the meeting of the Daughters of the Holy Cross.

The Supply Department, Mrs. T. M. DuBose, chairman, reported a valuable box sent to a minister, and one to a mountain mission.

The Flower chapter reported 500 printed cards, given by Mr. H. W. Cary, with appropriate verse, to be sent to the sick and suffering with the Altar flowers each Sunday.

The Business Women's chapter is mentioned here for the first time.

On May 9, 1924, the Parish House Fund of the Daughters of the Holy Cross amounted to $4,700.00. This to be sent to the Parish House Commitee as soon as the bonds could be sold.

Mrs. George Dial had for many years been doing a beautiful work with the women in the penitentiary and the girls in the State reformatory. She had a committee from the Daughters who worked with her, and the society for many years contributed to the Penitentiary Christmas Tree.

In 1925, the Training Chapter was formed to meet the need of bringing young women of the Church and newcomers of the parish into some organization which would train them in the work of the Church. Mrs. Christie Benet, as president of the Daughters had realized this need and with Dr. Phillips worked out the plans in which these women were drawn into a congenial group with a counselor. Here they learned of the Chapters of the Daughters and did special work of their own along lines in which they were interested. Mrs. Benet was the first counselor, then Mrs. M. C. Heath took over the work. Later Mrs. Bruce

W. Ravenel became counselor and under her leadership for the past nine years the chapter has done fine work, and become an outstanding chapter. From this chapter, after two years, members go into other chapters of their choice. This idea of a Training Chapter has attracted the attention of the National Church as a means of preparing young women and enlisting them in the Church's work.

For many years the Lenten mission study classes have been well attended. Mrs. W. K. Beckham has been the leader of the class for two years, 1936 and 1937, and has done a fine work in interesting and educating the class members in the Church's mission.

Mrs. James A. Cathcart was a very active president and under her leadership the society grew, and work in all departments was carried on with success. The Church Service League had been given up as a national church branch at the meeting of the convention in 1925 and that year Dr. Phillips asked that the Daughters and the Auxiliary come together as one. This was agreed to under the name "Daughters of the Holy Cross Unit of the Woman's Auxiliary." This was done with no sacrifice on the part of either society; each had a definite work. The same organization the Daughters had been using would be carried on. Mrs. John T. Sloan, Sr. was president of the Auxiliary. The Daughters made up the larger society, so their president became president of the whole. Uniting the women of the Church in one organization to carry on the Church's work in the five fields was a progressive step, in harmony both with modern organization and the old, old ideal of unity.

The budget for this year was $1,053.00. The society had agreed to raise $500.00 to equip the kitchen in the new parish house. This was to be raised by personal contributions, the gift raised to be placed on the plate on Trinity Sunday at the Church service.

The constitution had been changed so that the president would take office in January and not September, so Mrs. Cathcart served until January 1927. At that time the budget was $2,310.00, a great increase.

Mrs. Gadsden Shand had served one year as president in 1906; this was her second term. Changes had been made and this was a period of adjustment. The Board with departmental heads and

Chapter chairmen now decided on questions to be presented to the whole society. Departmental meetings were held and programs of educational value were presented. These took the place of the old general meetings so long the custom. These changes were thought necessary as the society had grown so large. The Chapters worked now independently of the whole society. The Lenten offering was still used in part for the support of two beds at Ridgewood and the remainder went this year to outfit the choir.

A gift of $50.00 was left to the Daughters by Mrs. John S. Reynolds for the educational fund.

The Door of Hope Chapter was abandoned in 1928 in view of the fact that the King's Daughters had taken it over. Before Mrs. A. S. Gaillard retired as chairman she turned over to Miss Finnstrom a personal gift of $85.00—money made by the chapter. It was given in appreciation of the life of service of Miss Finnstrom.

The Daughters and the Church suffered a loss at this time January 2nd, 1929 when Jennie Guignard Gibbes died after a brief illness. She was a charter member and worked untiringly for the society. Through the years she had been an efficient chairman of almost every chapter, also treasurer and secretary and loving the Daughters as a whole so dearly no one chapter absorbed her interest. She was treasurer of the parish for over 30 years. No one loved Trinity Church and the Daughters of the Holy Cross more than Jennie Gibbes. The altar on Easter Sunday, 1929, was decorated in loving memory of one who had always insisted "we must have those lilies for the altar."

Mrs. Moultrie Hutchinson as president took the chair at the January 1929 meeting.

The Daughters assumed part of the debt for the repair work on the interior of the Church. This was done by voluntary offering and with part of the Easter offering. Before the year was out $800.00 had been raised by the women for this purpose.

The Provincial Synod met in Trinity at this time and the supper committee did a splendid piece of work. This chapter which had for years been very active was able to function with great efficiency since the new kitchen in the parish house had been completely furnished. Mrs. Christie Benet had been deeply interested in this work.

The Synod had elected one of our members, Mrs. James R. Cain, President of the Provincial Branch of the Woman's Auxiliary to the National Church.

The Church School Auxiliary is one of the newer chapters. It was organized October 21st, 1930 at Dr. Phillips' suggestion. The first chairman was Mrs. Harold Young. It was composed of young women, many of them coming from the Training Chapter. Their special work was aiding the Church School, visiting new-comers whose children were in the school, looking up children not attending regularly, arousing parents' interest, and in other ways giving help. Later the chapter added social service to its activities, and now does work for the Door of Hope and visits in St. Matthew's Mission. This chapter helped to equip the room for the baby class in Church School, and gave to that class a lovely creche in memory of a member, Mrs. John Hopkins (Mary Dickerson), a former chairman who died in 1936.

Forty Thanksgiving baskets were sent to the poor in 1930 and the church was beautifully decorated for the service. In January 1931, these officers were installed: Miss Amelia Tompkins, president; Mrs. R. Beverley Sloan, vice-president; Mrs. S. C. Rhame, secretary; Mrs. O. Lee Gordon, assistant secretary; Mrs. C. T. Graydon, treasurer; Mrs. David G. Ellison, assistant treasurer; Mrs. Frank Schirmer, U. T. O. Custodian. The above list will give an idea of the officers now required for the Daughters of the Holy Cross Unit of the Woman's Auxiliary.

Mrs. Stephen Taber, a trained social worker conducted a class in Christian Social Service. The class took up social conditions in Columbia and Richland County.

A committee was appointed to appear before the Richland County delegation to ask for fire protection at the Girls' Reformatory.

The Woman's Exchange gave their final report at a meeting in February 1931, and turned over a balance $4,341.00. Mrs. J. J. Seibels recommended this sum be set aside for the organ fund.

Mrs. K. G. Finlay now succeeded Mrs. Benet as chairman of the supper chapter.

All women of the Church at this time were called to help with "The Christmas Shop" a city-wide project of the Associated

Charities, planned to help feed and clothe the poor of the community at this critical time. Mrs. Carroll Jones and Mrs. Malcolm Miller acted for Trinity Church on the central committee, the Charity chapter having a definite part in the work.

The Board at this time recommended to the Daughters that the society as a whole meet only three times a year but the recommendation was refused by a vote of a large majority of the society.

At this time the Daughters of the Holy Cross Unit of the Woman's Auxiliary suffered the loss of a devoted member, Mrs. Arthur de Jersey, and expressed "admiration of her life of loving, unstinted sacrifice and service; her grasp of the things of spirit and her boundless generosity."

Mrs. R. Beverley Sloan began her term in the dark month of January 1933, when depression was at its worst. Soon after this, all banks were closed and the society's money locked up. Mrs. Sloan stressed the idea that with little money to work with we could still give more of service, prayer and the best of our personalities. No new work could be taken up. Mrs. Sloan says her effort was to give the women a broader outlook. She stressed the spiritual side of the work.

The minutes of this time record the loss of the society of a former president, Mrs. Robert Moorman (Lessie Talley). "She had served the Daughters with devotion through long years of service—the third gold-star president."

In 1933 (December), Mrs. Sloan planned a Christmas meeting, and with Mrs. Fisher's help it was beautifully presented. The Christmas story was read, carols were sung, and the Christmas work of the chapters shown or explained, the Christmas trees for Ridgewood Camp, stockings filled, flowers for the "shut-ins" and so forth.

Mrs. Morris Lumpkin became president, January 1933. She had not served as vice-president, so hers was a more difficult undertaking. She was a most gracious and efficient officer doing everything possible to bring the women into closer fellowship. Her generosity was greatly appreciated. The two outstanding accomplishments of her term were the recovering of the cushions of the Church and organization of the Lebanon chapter.

The money for the cushions was contributed to by many of the chapters, raised by entertainments and special gifts, Mrs. Lumpkin making the final accomplishment possible by her own gift.

The Lenten offering in 1936 was voted to "Parish and the Missions of the Church." For the first time in 27 years no part went to the work at Ridgewood Camp. Sixty dollars for this work was given from the budget.

A patient at this time occupied the bed maintained by the Daughters of the Holy Cross. To keep this ill woman at the camp, the Tuberculosis chapter, Mrs. William Elliott, chairman, doubled in size and redoubled in efforts, raised the needed funds, and continues to carry on the anti-tuberculosis work so long a vital and inspiring part of the work of the society.

The Daughters of the Holy Cross Unit of the Woman's Auxiliary at this time rejoiced in the election of our former president as President of the Diocesan Branch of the Woman's Auxiliary, Mrs. R. Beverley Sloan.

For some years the Syrian women of the congregation of Trinity have been members and affiliates of the church. At the suggestion of the Rector a meeting was called of all those interested and desirous of forming a group and uniting with the women's organization of the Church and furthering its noble work. This meeting was held May 3, 1935. Dr. Phillips explained its purpose and helped with the founding of the chapter. Its first officers were Mrs. Z. J. Siokos, chairman; Miss Athalene Wackym, vice-chairman; Miss Olga Sabagga, secretary; and Mrs. Pete Papajohn, treasurer.

The suggestion by the chairman that the chapter be named "Lebanon" was unanimously approved. It numbers 23 members. As a further connecting link and in accord with Dr. Phillips' suggestion, the chairman, after much correspondence between inspection and agricultural bureas here and abroad, succeeded in obtaining a small cedar of Lebanon from Mount Lebanon, Syria. It was planted on Good Friday, 1937 in Trinity's churchyard, in the presence of a gathering of interested friends.

Since its founding, the Lebanon chapter has held monthly meetings at the homes of different members and has gladly accepted a share of the duties and work of the parish, and has made generous contributions to funds being raised by the Daughters.

The Altar has been served through all the years by faithful women of the Church. The names of Miss Colie Goodwin, Mrs. Thomas K. (Anna) Legare and Mrs. Charles Dwight are recalled as among those who ministered there when the Woman's Guild had charge. Later Miss Carrie Berry organized the Altar Chapter. There are many who have served faithfully through the years past. Some in the chapter today have worked there for ten to twelve years, others have been added in recent years. Theirs is a year-round job. The chapter is divided into groups of four who have charge of all services for one week at a time. The present chapter is as follows: Mrs. Alex King, chairman; Mrs. K. G. Finlay, Mrs. John Prioleau, Mrs. Legare Inglesby, Mrs. J. M. Cantey, Mrs. T. C. Lucas, Mrs. George LaFaye, Miss Laura Gulick, Mrs. T. C. Brown, Mrs. F. B. Fitch, Mrs. Wm. Shand, Mrs. Richard Singleton, Mrs. E. M. Kaminer, Mrs. Frank Graham, Mrs. O. B. Mayer and Mrs. T. J. Hopkins.

No account of the women of Trinity Church would be complete without some special mention of Miss Carrie Berry. She was chairman of this chapter for more than 20 years and trained the younger women in the work. With her it was a service of love and devotion and this spirit she passed on to those who worked with her at the altar.

She was always glad to explain to the children of the church the meaning of the service and show them the communion service, always trying to impress them with a feeling of reverence. She lived what she taught. Many in the congregation feel that "Miss Carrie's" spirit is never far from the church she loved so well.

January 1937, Mrs. W. Bedford Moore, Jr., became president with the following organization:

DAUGHTERS OF THE HOLY CROSS UNIT OF THE WOMAN'S AUXILIARY OFFICERS

President—Mrs. W. Bedford Moore, Jr., 1424 Washington St.
Vice-President—Mrs. Bruce W. Ravenel, 610 Elliott St.
Secretary—Mrs. H. A. Smith, Belt Line Rd., Kilbourne Park
Assistant Secretary—Miss Frances Sylvan, 4202 Main St.
Treasurer—Mrs. J. B. Murphy, 1014 Laurens St.
Assistant Treasurer—Mrs. Chas. I. Dial, 3626 Wilmot Ave.
U. T. O. Custodian—Mrs. Hope Lumpkin, 2222 Terrace Way

REV. KIRKMAN G. FINLAY, D. D.
Rector, 1907-1921
Bishop Co-adjutor, Diocese of S. C., 1921
First Bishop of Diocese of Upper S. C., 1922-

I—Missions and Church Extension Department

Chairman—Mrs. K. G. Finlay, 1717 Green St.

1. *Altar Chapter Chairman*—Mrs. Alex King, 1315 Blanding St.
2. *Business Women's Chapter Chairman*—Mrs. James R. McKenzie.
3. *Chancel Chapter Chairman*—Mrs. Thomas W. Waters, 1529 Pendleton St.
4. *Churchyard Chapter Chairman*—Mrs. A. E. Legare, 1314 Senate St.
5. *Choir Chapter Chairman*—Mrs. William Furtick, 1212 Pendleton St.
6. *Church Home Orphanage*—Mrs. George L. Dick, Charles-Edward Apts.
7. *Interracial Relations Committee*—Mrs. Jas. R. Cain, 631 Pickens St.
8. *Lebanon Chapter Chairman*—Mrs. Chris Athans, 1102 Price Ave.
9. *Offering of Life Committee*—Mrs. Jas. R. Cain, 631 Pickens St.
10. *Visiting Chapter Chairman*—Mrs. F. B. Fitch, 116 Harden St.

II—Religious Education Department

Chairman—Mrs. George A. Buchanan, Jr., 2220 Lee St.

1. *Church School Auxiliary Chairman*—Mrs. B. W. Kendall, 1810 Enoree Ave.
2. *Training Chapter Chairman*—Mrs. J. Henry Averill, 304 S. Waccamaw Ave.

III—Christian Social Service Department

Chairman—Mrs. William A. Crary, Jr., 1800 Wheat St.

1. *Charity Chapter Chairman*—Mrs. J. M. Atkinson, Dentsville
2. *Church Periodical Chapter Chairman*—Miss Isabelle Townsend
3. *Flower Chapter Chairman*—Mrs. M. C. Heath, Heathwood
4. *Ridgewood Camp Chapter Chairman*—Mrs. William Elliott, Jr., 1819 Pendleton St.
5. *Supper Chapter Chairman*—Mrs. C. T. Graydon, 1110 Barnwell St.
6. *Telephone Committee*—Mrs. Edgar T. Cato, Keenan Apts.

IV—SUPPLY DEPARTMENT

Chairman—Mrs. Arthur McIver Griffin, 1900 Heyward St.

V—PUBLICITY DEPARTMENT

Chairman—Mrs. Frank Dana, Heathwood

1. *Religious Publications Committee Chairman*—Mrs. Owen Riley, 1732 Maplewood Drive

This record of the work of the women of Trinity Church in these many years may be summed up by those words in St. Matthew, 25th Chapter "I was an hungered and ye gave me meat, I was thirsty and ye gave me drink, I was a stranger and ye took me in: Naked and ye clothed me. I was sick and ye visited me, I was in prison and ye came unto me—Inasmuch as ye have done it unto one of the least of these my brethren ye have done it unto me." The women who follow after may take the charge of St. Paul to Timothy to, "trust not in uncertain riches, but in the living God who giveth us richly all things to enjoy." That they do good, that they be rich in good works.

PRESIDENTS OF THE DAUGHTERS OF THE HOLY CROSS

1894—Miss Mary Stoney
1895-1901—Mrs. William McBurney Sloan—Gold Star
1901-1904—Mrs. Christopher FitzSimons
1904-1906—Miss Louly Shand
1906-1907—Mrs. Gadsden E. Shand
1907-1909—Mrs. A. B. Knowlton
1909-1911—Mrs. Frank G. Tompkins—Gold Star
1911-1912—Mrs. Charles H. Barron
1912-1913—Mrs. Edmund N. Joyner
1913-1915—Mrs. Tucker H. Fisher
1915-1917—Mrs. Robert Moorman—Gold Star
1917-1919—Mrs. James H. Fowles
1919-1920—Mrs. David G. Ellison
1920-1922—Mrs. H. Bland Hammond—Unit Church Service League
1922-1924—Mrs. Christie Benet
Oct. Jan.
1924-1927—Mrs. James A. Cathcart—Branch, Woman's Auxiliary

1927-1929—Mrs. Gadsden E. Shand
1929-1931—Mrs. Moultrie B. Hutchinson
1931-1933—Miss Amelia Tompkins
1933-1935—Mrs. R. Beverley Sloan
1935-1937—Mrs. Morris C. Lumpkin
1937-   —Mrs. W. Bedford Moore, Jr.

MEN'S ORGANIZATIONS

In the spring of 1913 the Rector of the parish, the Rev. Kirkman G. Finlay, felt the need of an organization for men of the parish. In April of that year he gathered a group together and organized the Men's Club of Trinity Church. The charter members numbered 35. The customary officers were elected and the constitution was drawn, setting forth the purposes of the organization. These were: First, to promote fellowship among the members; second, to discuss problems of interest to the membership; and, third, to undertake some constructive work of a religious nature.

The meetings of the Club were held once a month and the gatherings were of an informal nature. They furnished a fine medium for getting the men of the parish together and giving them an opportunity of becoming better acquainted. The Club filled a long-felt want in the life of the parish. The records of the Club unfortunately were lost, so it is impossible to give names of the officers. The Club had the distinction of being the first organization of its kind in South Carolina. Later other churches in the Diocese and churches of other communions formed similar organizations.

One of the outstanding results of the constructive work of the Club in its early days was the interest developed in the Church Home Orphanage at York. From the Club grew the Men's Orphanage Association of Trinity Parish. The dues of $3.00 were paid to the Association and transmitted to the Orphanage. The object of the Association was, "to study the needs, to strive by systematic efforts to advance the interest of the Church Home Orphanage, and to assist in an anual pilgrimage to York." The Association was able to help in completing the purchase of a house and additional acreage for the Orphanage.

In April 1922, the Association numbered 110 members. Duncan C. Ray was for many years president and remained active in the office until his death. He was succeeded by H. J. Gregg with C. Gadsden Guignard as vice-president and secretary, both of whom served for many years. Among those actively connected with the Association were J. Nelson Frierson, John P. Thomas, Jr. and others.

BOYS' CLUBS

In October, 1920, under the leadership of Rev. Mr. Finlay a troop of Boy Scouts was organized with Trinity church as sponsor. The place of meeting was then Satterlee Hall, and is now in the troop's own room in the present parish house. Dr. J. Bruce Coleman was the first Scoutmaster.

Since its organization, several hundred boys have been members of Troop 14, as this group was numbered in the list of troops in this area. These boys have been members of all religious faiths. Several years the Troop won first place in the city-wide jamboree, and has many other trophies won in various sports and in Scouting. From Troop 14 have come 36 Eagle Scouts. The Troop also has qualified for the Scout Church Award.

Trinity parish also sponsors the Senior Scout program and set up the first Sea Scout crew in this Scout area. The Sea Scouts of Trinity are under the leadership of George V. Sumner as Skipper.

Following Dr. Coleman, those who have served as Scoutmasters have been: John A. Manning, Wm. C. Coker, Wyndham Manning, John A. Manning again, J. B. Caughman, James Y. Perry, J. Ellis Craps, J. B. Caughman again, Leon Keaton, James R. Gibson, H. Bland Hammond, Jr., Harold E. Jervey.

Assistant Scoutmasters have been: John Roddey, J. M. Cantey, Jr., Jas. H. Fowles, Jr., H. Bland Hammond, Jr., Eugene C. Cathcart, Leon Keaton, John Payne, J. Ellis Craps, Loren Epton, James R. Gibson, Wallace Martin, Williams Bryan.

A group of men of the parish serve as a Troop committee to forward the work of the Troop and to serve as a link between parish and Scouts. This committee has been composed of men with special interest in boys' work, and furnishes one of the most valuable channels of expression for the Men's organization. Those who have served on this committee have been: J. M. Bell, Jas. H. Fowles, Jas. A. Cathcart, A. B. Owings, Rev. H. D. Phillips, E. L. Allison, N. H. Clarkson, Landon C. Jones, C. P. Seabrook, Geo. E. Lafaye, T. Fraser Dial, Bruce Walker Ravenel, Edgar T. Cato, Jas. G. Holmes, Geo. A. Saussy, Chas. H. Moorefield, Christopher FitzSimons, W. S. Reamer, Jr., Walter H. Sims, Dr. Wm. Weston, Jr., Lemuel Scott, Alfred Goodwyn.

Reaching some 120 boys, the Scouting program of Trinity is, next to the Church school, the largest and most influential work for boys engaged in by the parish. Co-ordinating and unifying this whole program for the well-rounded development of boyhood, is Bruce W. Ravenel. Mr. Ravenel acts as liason officer between Scouts, Sea Scouts and Cubs, linking the several units with each other, with the Troop committee and with the parish. It was Mr. Ravenel, too, who organized the Sea Scout troop and the Cubs, these latter active until recently.

The members of the Club rendered invaluable service in connection with the Every Member Canvass.

In 1922, with the advent of the new Rector, Dr. Henry D. Phillips, the Club was meeting each month though it was realized that the get-together feature of the Club was waning because of the increased number and interest in the various service clubs. Therefore, efforts were made to give definite work to men in the organization.

After many experiments, in 1934, the Men's Club was reorganized. The name was changed to the Men's Organization —inclusive rather than exclusive, as the name "Club" seemed to mean to some. In the reorganization the effort was made to overcome weak spots which had been recognized during the life of the organization.

A board of directors numbering 16 and with the Rector as chairman was selected. The members of the board were to serve two years except that at the end of the first year of the organization, one-half were to retire. Those retiring were determined by lot. The old board made nominations for the vacancies and these were ratified by the Organization at large. The board of directors elects its officers. The first president under the new organization was Charles M. Schmidt. The board was divided into committees as follows: Every Member Canvass; Membership and Visiting; Youth; Service; and Program.

The Organization continues under this general set-up. The second president was Kirkman Finlay. The board is made up of interested chairmen and is responsible for the policy and direction of the activities of the Organization. The Organization now numbers 175. At quarterly yearly meetings a delightful supper is served. These meetings have not only been pleasant social occasions but have been of immeasurable value. The programs are built upon some phase of Church work.

The Church Service Committee has done a fine piece of work in promoting and sponsoring the Lenten services on Thursday evenings and in making possible a broadcast of the Church services once a month. The Youth Committee has been contacting and sponsoring the Scouts.

Below is given a list of the officers of the Men's Club and Organization taken from the available records.

MEN'S CLUB

1922-1923—*President*—J. B. Coleman
    Vice-President—S. A. Irby
1923-1924—*President*—Carroll Jones
    Vice-President—Jas. H. Fowles
1924-1925—*President*—R. B. Sloan
    Vice-President—Hunter Gibbes
1925-1926—*President*—R. B. Sloan
    Vice-President—Edgar Cato
1926-1927—*President*—Edgar Cato
    Vice-President—Frank Dana
1927-1928—*President*—W. M. Shand
    Vice-President—S. T. Pender
1928-1929—*President*—David G. Ellison
    Vice-President—S. T. Pender
1929-1930—*President*—Arthur McI. Griffin (January 13, 1929)
    President—S. T. Pender (April 14, 1929)
    Vice-President—R. E. Carwile
1930-1931—*President*—O. Lee Gordon
    Vice-President—H. Gordon Kenna
1931-1932—
1932-1933—
1933-1934—*President*—Hunter Gibbes
    Vice-President—
1934-1935—*President*—Chas. M. Schmidt
    Vice-President—W. J. Keenan, Jr.
1935-1936—*President*—Clark Waring
    Vice-President—Kirkman Finlay
1936-1937—*President*—Kirkman Finlay

GIFTS, MEMORIALS AND LEGACIES

The question is often asked, "Why have memorials? Why not put the money into conserving human lives and into educational opportunities rather than into monuments of wood and stone?" The answer is that, history is preserved in monuments and buildings. Before the written word, often only a stone or a pile of rocks marked some historic event. It is as true today as then.

So gifts and memorials to Trinity Church show the progress of her growth and bear testimony to many faithful soldiers and servants of Christ who left the rich heritage we possess in our splendid parish. Ours be the responsibility to bear the torch as they have done!

Since documentary history of the congregation prior to February 17th, 1865, was destroyed with the rectory at the time of the burning of Columbia, much that is here recorded has been handed down as tradition; and this record is an effort to preserve such while those who have received the story from the past are here to pass it on.

Gifts

Trinity congregation was organized in 1812 and the cornerstone of the first edifice was laid March 7, 1814.

Mr. Moorman, in his *History and Traditions of Trinity Church*, says:

"It is not certain how our Parish acquired the two acres of land upon which our present Church, Parish House and Cemetery are located, because the records of conveyance of our county were destroyed, but tradition has it that the northern acre in which the first church edifice was built, and where the cemetery now is, was given by a widow named Smythe in 1813; and the southern acre (according to Col. A. R. Taylor) as purchased from Col. Gregg by Colonel Wade Hampton (father of Governor Hampton). Col. Gregg sold the lot on condition that it should never be used for a burying ground, which condition has been faithfully complied with. Mrs. Smythe's gift also had a condition, so tradition says. She wished her family to be buried under the grand old live oak in the churchyard. By some mistake we did not keep the faith with her, and someone else was buried there. So indignant was Mrs. Smythe, that she withdrew from the congregation."

J. P. Thomas, as secretary, in a report to Trinity congregation on March 30, 1891, says:

"In accordance with a resolution passed at your annual meeting, I have attempted to gather together such records of the parish as were accessible." From these records I obtained much information. In connection with the gift of Colonel Hampton, this letter from his daughter is of such interest as to be included in this article.

"Millwood, April 14, 1891.

Dear Mr. Thomas:

I did not mention the lot in my note, as no information was asked about it, but as Mrs. Bachman inquired of us the donor, I wish to express our indebtedness to old Trinity—In return for this gift of my father, the Vestry very liberally gave him the privilege of marking off as large a lot in the churchyard as he desired, and the extensive graveyard now owned by our family was thus given by the church.

"And years before, in the early days of Trinity, a pew was given to my grandfather, and when the present church was built, the gift was transferred to one of the desirable pews for my grandmother, and in later years, my brother, General Hampton, has enjoyed the privilege of a free pew. Thus you see there have been many acts of liberality from Trinity towards our family, and in recording our gifts, we should be glad to know that alongside of them mention be made of Trinity's gifts to us.

With kind regards,
Yours truly,
KATE HAMPTON."

"Gen. Wade Hampton the older," quoting again from Mr. Moorman, "contributed $2,000.00 and the organ to the first building. Generous sums were also contributed by Gen. C. C. Pinckney, Messrs. Elias Horry and Peter Smith of Charleston. Mrs. Mary Gregorie and Mrs. Sarah Russell (also of Charleston) assisted in the adornment, and Hon. Elias Lynch Horry, presented the Communion plate consisting of flagon, chalice, and paten.

In 1834, Rev. Peter J. Shand, D. D., gave to the church a Prayer Book which was still in possession of the church a few years ago.

So much for the first little cruciform church where Dr. Shand began his rectorship.

The cornerstone of our present beautiful building was laid in 1846. It is said that the Hampton family offered to build it alone, but Dr. Shand insisted that the funds be raised by popular subscription, which was done. According to Mrs. Bachman the Hamptons contributed very handsomely to it.

All of the stained glass windows in the nave of the church, as well as the beautiful rose windows in the transepts were gifts of Gen. John S. Preston. A few of these have been replaced by modern memorial windows. (Mrs. Bachman and Mrs. Robert Shand remembered that the windows given by Mr. Preston came from Munich).

The marble Communion table was a gift from the Misses Hampton. (NOTE: When the table was enlarged the original marble was preserved.)

The three chancel chairs were given by Mrs. John S. Preston.

The marble tablets were given either by Mrs. Wade Hampton, Gov. Hampton's grandmother, or by Mrs. John Preston.

The marble font, a gift of Mrs. Wade Hampton, grandmother of Gov. Hampton, was designed by the great sculptor Powers. There were two fonts, both the work of Powers. The original one was one-half the size of the one now in use. As it was considered too small, Mr. Powers was persuaded to execute the larger one. After a few years the discarded font was given to Rev. Mr. McCullough. He used it several years in Spartanburg and from there he removed it to the Church of the Nativity in Union, S. C., where it now is. (It is said that the Prestons befriended Mr. Powers when he was a lad, and it was through their influence that Mrs. Hampton was enabled to get the second font made.)

A small marble Cross for the Altar was given by Mrs. Edward H. Heinitsh. It was the first cross on the altar, and was replaced by a large one given by Rev. J. H. Stringfellow, as a memorial to his sister—and at the request of Mrs. Heinitsh. Miss Carrie Berry said the cross in the Baptistry is the one given by Mrs. Heinitsh. Mr. Thomas in his report, said it was given to the Church of the Good Shepherd.

The first organ was the gift of Gen. Wade Hampton, grandfather of Gov. Hampton.

The finials to the church building were given by Colonel Wade Hampton, father of Gov. Hampton. These finials had an ornamental lead covering. At the time of the War between the States, the lead was taken off and melted into bullets for the use of the soldiers of the Confederacy.

The church bell was the gift of Gouveneur Morris Thompson at the time the church was built.

The crucifer Cross was the first permanent gift made by the Daughters of the Holy Cross to the church.

The large double doors at the west entrance to the church as well as the two doors to transepts were given by the Daughters of the Holy Cross, but the brass mountings were placed there later by the Vestry.

The two undesignated windows on the side of the west entrance were given by the Daughters of the Holy Cross, as well as the marble re-table.

The brass pulpit as given by the Chancel Chapter of the Guild. Much of the work and many gifts of this chapter were not in permanent form and cannot be listed, even if a record of them had been kept. They worked untiringly for the choir, furnishing and making many cottas and cassocks as well as buying music for the choir.

The seven-branched vesper candlesticks were given by Mrs. Charles M. Niles, wife of the Rector.

The two large chalices, ciborium, paten and two small cruets were made from old gold, silver and jewelry given by members of the congregation and assembled for that purpose by Dr. Niles.

Mrs. Louisa Logan made a gift of $5,000.00 to the church to be used for improvements. Some of the things done with this sum were: A much needed tin roof was put on the building; the ceiling of the Sanctuary was raised; a tiled floor was laid in the Sanctuary; the marble chancel rail was built; and the finials of the church were restored. They have since been rebuilt.

The small silver Cross on the old Credence Table in the Baptistry is a thank offering for the recovery of Charles Capers Satterlee, and was given by his mother.

The brass ewer is a thank offering given by Mrs. William M. Shand for her four children: Helen Coles Shand (Mrs. F. Barron Grier); William Munro Shand, Jr.; Louisa Ioor Shand (Mrs. Emmet L. Wingfield); and Mary Wright Shand.

The fence surrounding the church property was a gift from Mr. Charles McCreery.

A Prayer Book in the Baptistry has inscribed thereon:

A GIFT TO

TRINITY CHURCH

FROM

JOHN PIERPONT MORGAN

A. D. 1932

A small red leather hymnal for visiting clergy was given by the Altar Chapter, December 1, 1929. The names are written on the fly leaf as follows:

MRS. K. G. FINLAY	MISS LAURA GULICK
MRS. E. C. McGREGOR	MRS. LEGARE INGLESBY
MRS. C. FITZSIMONS	MRS. JOHN G. PRIOLEAU
MRS. A. E. KING	MRS. F. B. FITCH
MRS. J. D. BELL	MRS. G. E. LAFAYE
MISS MARY HUGH MEIGHAN	MRS. J. M. CANTEY

The prayer book to the set is a memorial and is given under that head.

"In 1928 an anonymous donation was made to the church through the Rector, Dr. H. D. Phillips of $2,400.00 for the purpose of purchasing and installing in the church more suitable electric lighting fixtures" (from secretary's report). This gift provided for the first time in the life of the parish lighting that is beautiful, appropriate and adequate.

The new organ represents gifts from individuals as well as organizations, amounting to $14,778.37. Among the donors are: Mrs. Clark Waring, Mrs. Morris Lumpkin, the Daughters of the Holy Cross through the Woman's Exchange, the Organ Fund Committee, and other small groups and individuals.

Mrs. A. I. deJersey in 1929 gave the iron railing to the steps at the south entrance to the church.

M. C. Heath donated the large safe now used in the Rector's office.

In July, 1930, W. S. Reamer made a gift of $1,000.00 to the church to be used at the discretion of the Vestry, who later passed a resolution to add to it a legacy left by Mr. Reamer and designate it as the Reamer Fund.

SATTERLEE HALL

In June, 1902, our Rector, the Rev. Churchill Satterlee, announced the gift of $1,000.00 toward the building of a Parish House, which had been a dream of his since coming to Trinity parish. It was learned later that Mrs. Susan DesPortes was the donor. In 1907 private contributions, including the All Saints and Easter offerings, most of which were given by friends of the Rev. Mr. Satterlee outside of the state and in special memory of our beloved Rector, amounted to $6,000.00. Thus the first parish house was begun and the first unit—the Sunday school room was built and called Satterlee Hall in honor of the founder.

TRINITY PARISH HOUSE

In the march of progress the need for larger quarters resulted in the present beautiful parish house. Many contributions were given in memory of loved ones. The list appears farther on in this sketch.

LEGACIES

No assembled list of the legacies left to Trinity Church could be obtained and what is here recorded has been gathered here and there, and cannot claim to be complete.

Mrs. Mary Parr, by her will dated July 3, 1844, made the following bequest:

"I give and bequeath to the Rev. P. J. Shand, Rector of the Protestant Episcopal Church in Columbia aforesaid, called Trinity Church, the sum of Three Thousand (3,000) Dollars, In Trust to apply or invest the same in any way and manner he may consider meet and proper for the use and benefit of said Trinity Church. And I desire that the said legacy may be paid over to the said Peter J. Shand, for said purpose, within one year from my decease."

In a codicil to her will dated March 24, 1848, Mrs. Parr made the following provisions:

"I do hereby annex as a condition to my legacy to the Protestant Episcopal Church in Columbia, called Trinity Church, that the vestry and wardens of the said church shall from time to time keep my family vault in the cemetery of said church in good repair, as the same may require it. And it is my will and desire that my Executors, before paying over said legacy to said church, should obtain from the vestry and wardens then in office a pledge or promise, or writing, for themselves or their successors in office to have the said vault attended to whenever the same may need them."

This legacy was paid to Rev. P. J. Shand, November 31, 1848.

Miss Lucy Green left a legacy of $3,000.00 to the vestry and wardens of Trinity Church, Columbia, the interest to be used for the care of the burying ground, and in providing employment for the poor of the parish of Trinity church. The last mentioned was in memory of her mother. The legacy was paid to the vestry and wardens on July 2, 1900.

Miss Sophie Carroll left to the Rector and vestry of Trinity $1,000.00 to be invested and the interest to be used to care for the Carroll lot in perpetuity and "also in aiding the poor people of the Parish." This legacy was paid in 1924.

A legacy of $12,000.00 was left Trinity church by Mrs. Louisa Logan. This was undesignated and was used by the vestry in the purchase of the present rectory.

Mrs. George Lippard Baker's legacy reads as follows:

"I give to the vestry of Trinity Church, Columbia, S. C., in loving memory of my husband, who was for years an earnest and devoted member of this church, the sum of $12,500 to be used by said Vestry for the benefit of Trinity Church for the adornment or improvement of the church proper, and a fitting tablet shall be erected in the church commemorating the bequest as a memorial to my husband, George Lippard Baker."

The memorial stand and credence table fulfilled terms of the bequest. (Found later under Memorials.)

George Xepapas left to Trinity church a legacy of $100.00 undesignated.

Mrs. Louisa Shand (Mrs. Robert W. Shand) left a legacy of $100.00 for the organ fund.

W. S. Reamer left a legacy of $5,000.00 to Trinity church to be used at the discretion of the vestry.

MEMORIALS

Many of the gifts to our Church and parish house are designated as memorials. The list is as complete as it was possible for the writer to compile, but there are doubtless omissions and inaccuracies.

TABLETS

The mural tablet in the Baptistry is a memorial to Rev. Peter Shand, D. D., Rector of Trinity Church for more than 50 years. It was placed there by the congregation.

The tablet in the southern transept is a memorial to Maximilian LaBorde, M. D., senior, who died November 6, 1873, warden of the church for many years. Given by the congregation.

The bronze bas-relief near the west entrance to the church is a memorial to Benjamin Walter Taylor, 1834-1905, given by his children. Dr. Taylor was for many years warden of the church.

Two other bronze mural tablets commemorate the lives of soldiers and patriots of the congregation. One records the names of those who gave their lives for the cause of the Confederacy, and bears this inscription: "Hold up the glory of thy dead, Carolina." The other bears tribute to the young men of Trinity Parish who rendered definite service to our government in the World War. Both tablets were erected by the congregation.

WINDOWS

The large memorial window in the Sanctuary is in memory of Rev. Peter Shand, D. D. Tradition says each person baptized by Dr. Shand had a share in this memorial. At any rate it was given by the congregation.

The stained glass window in the Baptistry is a memorial to Hugh Smith Thompson, 1836-1904 and Elizabeth Clarkson Thompson, 1840-1909; given by their children and grandchildren.

The windows at the west entrance are memorials to: Jane Beverley Sloan; James Mercier Gibbes; Annie Sloan Beverley; and Ethel Hope Evans. The first was given by her husband, Col. John T. Sloan; the other two by their families; and the one to Ethel Hope Evans was given by the Daughters of the Holy Cross.

The memorial windows in the nave of the church are to:

GEORGE L. BAKER

SOMETIME VESTRYMAN

27 JULY 1862   16 JAN. 1924

This was given by his wife.

REV. HENRY D. PHILLIPS, D. D.
Rector, January 1, 1922-

EMMA GUIGNARD GAMBRILL

7 MAY 1847 25 NOV. 1928

AND

DAVIDGE GAMBRILL

8 AUG. 1836 14 DEC. 1905

Given by their niece, Mary G. Jenkins.

MORRIS LUMPKIN

5 DEC. 1888 22 MAY 1933

VESTRYMAN. A LOVER OF CHURCH MUSIC

Given by his wife.

The stained glass window in the auditorium of the parish house is in memory of Paul Ellis Moseley. It had a place corresponding to this in the first Satterlee Hall. Given by his parents, Mr. and Mrs. George Moseley.

The beautiful leaded glass window in the reception room of the parish house was the gift of Mrs. Clark Waring as a memorial to her son:

CLARK WARING, JR.

1887-1909

A SOLDIER OF THE CROSS

FURNITURE

The hand-carved walnut choir stalls were given in loving memory of Rev. Churchill Satterlee, Rector of Trinity parish, by the Daughters of the Holy Cross.

The Altar rail is a memorial to Major Edwin Whipple Seibels, given by his sons.

The eagle lectern is a memorial to:

ALEXANDER NICHOLAS TALLEY, D. D.

JULY 6, 1897

Given by his family. Dr. Talley and Dr. Taylor served as wardens together for many years.

The litany desk was given by Colonel and Mrs. Wilie Jones in memory of their little daughter:

LUCY REAUX

SEPT. 3, 1890 APR. 1, 1893

(The lilies placed on the desk each year at Easter are also memorials).

The two prayer desks are memorials. One bears the name of:

ANNIE ISABELLA JONES

APRIL 10, 1816   JAN. 4, 1897

Given by her children and grandchildren. The other is in memory of:

ALICE GIBBES CHILDS

JUNE 11, 1853   OCT. 5, 1900

Given by her grandchildren.

The three memorial walnut hymn boards are:

IN MEMORY
OF
MRS. LOUISA DOROTHY LOGAN
AUG. 13, 1834   JAN. 14, 1921

NOTE: In view of the undesignated legacy given by Mrs. Logan the vestry placed this hymn board in the church as a visible token of appreciation of her devotion to Trinity.

IN MEMORIAM
SAMUEL ANTHONY IRBY
SEPT. 12, 1883   JAN. 26, 1935

Erected by his wife.

Given by his friends and comrades in grateful memory of:

ROBERT ELLIOTT GONZALES
SERGEANT MACHINE GUN CO.
SECOND SOUTH CAROLINA INFANTRY
APRIL 18, 1888
DEC. 19, 1916
DIED IN EL PASO, TEXAS

The memorial stand and credence table were placed by the vestry.

IN MEMORY
OF
GEORGE LIPPARD BAKER
AND
FRANK GUALDO FORD BAKER

The marker is on the memorial stand. This complies with the terms of the will, as stated under Legacies.

Upon the Memorial Stand is placed at the Sunday service the handsome red leather memorial book bearing this inscription:

SUSANNE COURTONNE HASKELL

WIFE OF

HARVEY NATHANIEL DAUS

BORN IN THIS PARISH

FEBRUARY 16, 1886

DIED IN CAMBRIDGE, MASS.

JANUARY 1, 1918

GIVEN BY HER SISTER

MRS. CHRISTIE BENET

The memorial cabinet in the choir room:

GIVEN IN LOVING MEMORY

OF

CAROLINE MORRISON BERRY

APRIL 24, 1859   MARCH 10, 1936

For many years chairman of the Altar Chapter and
of the Churchyard Chapter

"Blessed are they that dwell in Thy House
They will be always praising Thee."—Ps. 84:4

This is the outward expression of love and appreciation from the Altar Chapter and other friends of "Miss Carrie" in the congregation.

SILVER AND BRASS

The large Cross on the Altar is a memorial to Augustus Barton Knowlton, given by his parents, Dr. and Mrs. A. B. Knowlton. It replaced the marble cross given by Mr. Stringfellow as a memorial to his sister.

The eucharistic candlesticks are a memorial to Maximillian LaBorde, given by his daughter, Ellen Carroll LaBorde, and the altar vases are a memorial to Elizabeth Carroll LaBorde.

Miss Carrie Berry thought they were given by Miss Ellen LaBorde and she was told that they and the candlesticks were made from family silver.

The brass stand and Prayer Book used on the Altar are in memory of Ethel Hope Evans, given by her parents, Dr. and Mrs. W. E. Evans.

NOTE: Ethel died just after Dr. Evans was called to Columbia, and before the family moved here.

Alms Basins and Plates

The alms basin is a memorial to Halcott Pride Green, and was given by the congregation.

The four alms plates are memorials to: Robert Wilson Gibbes, vestryman and warden of the church for many years; Robert Wallace Shand, vestryman and warden for 24 years; Allen Jones, vestryman and warden for 12 years; and Davidge Gambrill. They were presented by the families of the above named.

The small alms plates are in memory of Virginia Taylor Green, and Lucy Jones Green, given by their families.

The two silver alms plates used in the primary department of the Church school are memorials to Nancy Hart (1907-1913), given by her parents, Dr. and Mrs. O. Frank Hart, and Henry Plummer Bain (1899-1905), given by his parents.

The carved walnut alms plate is a memorial to Hampden Brooks Shannon, given by his parents.

Shell and Stopper

The baptismal shell is a memorial to Elizabeth Berrien Screven given by her aunt, Miss Sophie Carroll.

The silver stopper in the Font was given by her parents in memory of Emily Margaret Brooks. The stopper was stolen but has been replaced.

Chalice and Flagon

The small chalice and flagon are a memorial to Governor John Peter Richardson, given by his wife.

Prayer Books and Hymnals

The small red leather Prayer Book for visiting clergy is marked:

In Memoriam
Oliver Franklin Hart, son of
O. Frank and Nancy C. Hart

Note: The hymnal to match was the one mentioned in Gifts, and donated by the Altar Chapter.

The red leather Prayer Book and Hymnal on the memorial Prayer Desk to Mrs. Annie Iredell Jones are also memorials. The inscription reads as follows:

To the Glory of God
In Loving Memory of our
Grand-parents
Cadwallader Jones
1813-1899
Annie Isabella Iredell Jones
1816-1877

Dec. 1, 1929

The handsome red leather litany book on the litany desk was given by his wife:

In Memory of
of
Wilie Jones
1850-1936

The white book mark for the litany prayer desk is a memorial to Francis Thomas Parker, given by his wife.

Contributions as Memorials

Many of the contributions to our present parish house were given as memorials and the names presented on Easter Sunday 1920. It was understood that a mural tablet with these inscribed would be placed in the parish house. The list is given below with the names of the donors:

Julia Rush Bachman—by Mrs. T. H. Fisher

John Bell—by Joseph and John Bell

Georgia Wright Bollin—by Mrs. J. H. Bollin and Mrs. H. Bland Hammond

Berrien Brooks, Jr. and Emily Margaret Brooks—by Mr. and Mrs. M. B. Brooks

Elizabeth A. Carroll—by Miss Sophie Carroll

Katherine Stewart Cathcart—by James A. Cathcart

Lewis Parke Chamberlayne—by Mrs. L. P. Chamberlayne

Lillian Bollin Ellison—by Mrs. J. H. Bollin and Mrs. H. Bland Hammond

Ellen S. Elmore—by Miss Cornelia Davidson

John Fisher—by Mrs. F. J. Dana
Cleland Huger FitzSimons—by Mrs. Christopher FitzSimons
Davidge Gambrill—by Mrs. Davidge Gambrill
Robert Wilson Gibbes, M. D.—by J. Wilson Gibbes
Allen J. Green—by Mrs. Allen Green
Allen Singleton Green—by Mrs. Singleton Green
Susan Guignard Jenkins—by Mary Gambrill Jenkins
Robert Elliott Gonzales—by W. E. and A. E. Gonzales
Abel A. Hutchinson—by Mr. and Mrs. M. B. Hutchinson
Alice Beverley Jones—by Mr. and Mrs. Carroll H. Jones
Maurice Herndon Moore—by Mr. and Mrs. Henry Fair
Mrs. W. P. Northrop—by Mrs. —— Gary
Heber Screven Reynolds, John Schreiner Reynolds, John Schrei-
    ner Reynolds, Jr.—by Mrs. J. S. Reynolds, Mrs. H. L.
    Forbes, and Miss Sarah E. Reynolds (Mrs. Amos E. Schar-
    bell)
Mrs. Badeia Sabbagha—by S. A. Sabbagha
Rev. Churchill Satterlee—There were three envelopes marked
    In Memoriam, Rev. Churchill Saterlee
    (NOTE: One contained a check from Miss Carrie Heyward)
Caroline Thompson Seibels—by J. T. Seibels
Martha Rutledge Singleton—by Mrs. Allen J. Green
John Trimmier Sloan—by R. Beverley Sloan
Mary Green Swaffield—by Fred Swaffield
Anna Heyward Taylor—by Dr. Julius H. Taylor
Mary Gibbes Thomas—by John P. Thomas, Jr.
Mary Sumter Waties Thomas—by John P. Thomas, Jr.
Fanny Parker Waties—by Miss Kate Waties

There have been from time to time gifts and memorials to
the church which are not included in this record, because they
were not of permanent form.

Mrs. F. G. Swaffield's beautiful floral designs placed on Easter
in the church as memorials to members of the congregation,
come under this group. They were works of art, and were designed when money was too scarce for permanent memorials.

Without the aid of Robert Moorman, the report of John P.
Thomas, Jr., and the help of Miss Carrie Berry, who carried
enshrined upon her heart many of the facts here given, this
chapter of our church history, however incomplete could not
have been written.

As Mr. Moorman so well stated in his *History and Traditions of Trinity Church*:

"We should be immensely grateful for the privilege of worshipping our Creator in beautiful Trinity, where the most sacred relations of our lives center. We should never forget that this precious heritage came absolutely without cost to our present members. Surely we are sufficiently appreciative to see that this beautiful edifice is materially and spiritually preserved for all who now or may hereafter enjoy the great privilege it offers."

TRINITY CHURCHYARD

In a very real sense Trinity Church of today rises from its past. From the memory and the spirit of those who have gone before, the church still draws inspiration and strength. The churchyard, where rest some of the founders of the parish, and many other faithful servants of Christ, who in their generation have given of themselves and their substance to church, city, state and nation, affords a lasting reminder of the heritage of duty, service and honor that is of the essence of the life of Trinity parish.

In the early days of the parish, burial lots were granted informally to pew-holders. The records of such transactions were destroyed by fire in 1865. A few deeds of burial spaces have been recorded since 1865. The actual graveyard is less than one acre, because the present church occupies a part of this space. The original land used for burial places was less than half an acre, as the first church building was in the northwest corner of the lot and there was at one time a small Sunday school building in the northeast corner.

In records of a vestry meeting held January 7, 1895, is found this:

"The matter of burial lots was discussed but it was deemed best that the management of same remain as formerly in the hands of the Rector and Wardens." A resolution was adopted requiring that in the future no fence or wall around any burial lot in Trinity Churchyard shall be erected which shall exceed eighteen inches in height. On April 13, 1895, the Vestry directed that a plat locating the burial lots in the Churchyard be made, and that Gadsden E. Shand be employed to do so. The Vestry donated a burial lot to Bishop Ellison Capers on April 15, 1895, the Bishop to select any available lot."

A map of the cemetery made by G. McDuffie Hampton hangs in the vestibule of Trinity Church. A more complete map is being made now by Gadsden E. Shand in which will be shown each grave and, as nearly as possible, the names of all persons buried in the church cemetery.

The magnificent live-oak tree in the graveyard, known as "The Sire Oak," was planted; it did not just happen to grow there. The Vestry has gone to considerable expense in preserving this wonderful tree. The late and beloved Miss Carrie Berry, who worked with such faithful care in the churchyard for 40 years, said that Miss Mary McCammon's mother remembered when Mr. Parr planted the tree and that he wanted to be buried under it, but later he had the vault built on the other side of the cemetery. It is the only one in the yard. It is told that when the last member of the Parr family was buried there by Dr. Peter Shand, the will requested that he should throw the key away. When Columbia was burned by Sherman, his men broke the marble door of the vault hoping to find treasure; but an iron door prevented further desecration.

In front of the vault are two beautiful cedars. Miss Carrie Berry said Judge Haskell told her they were brought from Lebanon by the gardener who brought and planted the rare trees in the Preston garden. She was sure the two large euonymus bushes in the yard came from Mount Lebanon. At the back of the church is a euonymus bush that came from Mount Vernon.

Tradition has always been that the beautiful ivy in the yard was originally brought from York Minster in England, the church after which Trinity is patterned. A member of the Brown family said the lovely dwarf English ivy in their lot was brought from England.

Enclosing the Clarkson lot is an interesting iron fence with handsome posts, cast after the war from Confederate guns at the old Shields' foundry.

Around the southeastern portion of the churchyard, just inside the iron fence, runs a "memory rose border,." planted by the Churchyard chapter in remembrance of workers who have passed on.

The graves in the churchyard which show the earliest dates are those of two infants of the Guignard family, interred in the old Guignard lot, and dated 1810. Since there was no parish organization and no graveyard on this property at this time, it is assumed that these two graves were removed from some other burying ground; perhaps at the time of the interment of the grandmother of these children, Elizabeth Sanders Guignard, "amiable consort" of John Gabriel Guignard. Mrs. Guignard, buried in 1814, was probably the first person buried in Trinity churchyard after the organization of the congregation of Trinity church.

Among those buried in our churchyard in the first years of its use was that intrepid Revolutionary leader, General Peter Horry. This gallant gentleman died Feburary 28, 1815, and was buried in the old Guignard lot. The stone that marks his grave is quite modest, and is now difficult to find, being almost hidden with ivy. It is marked by a bronze tablet placed by the Daughters of the American Revolution.

Back of the church is the Stark lot, where the stones are set in the brick wall and show dates of death earlier than the date of General Horry's death. It is quite certain that those persons were buried in the old Stark graveyard and that their gravestones were moved to Trinity churchyard within the last thirty-five years. The Stark graveyard was located where William Elliott now lives on Pendleton Street.

Another stone, to Mrs. Mary C. Mathiel, bears the date of 1811. This too, must have been moved to the churchyard, but from where is not known.

Ten of our clergy, including Bishop Ellison Capers, lie buried in Trinity churchyard. They are: the Rev. Peter J. Shand, the Rev. Charles Bruce Walker, the Rev. Robert Barnwell, the Rev. Thomas Boston Clarkson, the Rev. Robert Henry, the Rev. Napoleon B. Screven, and the Rev. Sanders Richardson Guignard.

Three soldiers of the American Revolution: Robert Stark, who served from 1775 to 1783; General Wade Hampton, who was a colonel of the American Revolution, and Brigadier-General of the War of 1812; General Peter Horry already mentioned.

Three Generals of the War between the States honor the soil also: Brigadier-General States Rights Gist, killed in the Battle of Franklin, Tenn., in 1864; Brigadier-General Ellison Capers, who is listed above as Bishop and Clergyman; and Lieutenant-General Wade Hampton, later Governor of South Carolina and United States Senator.

On Memorial Day 1937 the United Daughters of the Confederacy placed in our churchyard 63 flags to the honor of the soldiers of the Confederacy.

There lie here, too, veterans of the Spanish-American war and the World war.

Of statesmen, as well this square beside Trinity church, is the resting place. Four governors of South Carolina, besides General Hampton. The three Mannings, Richard Irvine Manning, who served 1824-1826; his son, John Laurence Manning, 1852-54; Richard Irvine Manning, who was our War governor and served 1915-1919; and Hugh Smith Thompson, 1882-1886.

Sleeping here also, are three presidents of the University of South Carolina. Dr. Thomas Cooper, friend of Thomas Jefferson, and second president of the South Carolina College; Dr. Robert Henry, and Dr. Maximilian LaBorde.

John Gabriel Guignard, Treasurer and Surveyor-General of the State of South Carolina, under whose direction the City of Columbia was laid out, was buried here in 1822.

Near the Gervais Street gate is buried one of the most eminent scientists that South Carolina has produced, Dr. Robert W. Gibbes.

Others who should be noted are: Alexander Herbemont, consul to the city of Geneva; and his father, Nicholas Herbemont, professor of Languages at the South Carolina College; and Colonel Joseph Matthews, superintendent of Arsenal Academy.

Dr. Thomas Jefferson Goodwyn, who was Mayor of Columbia when the city was burned by Sherman, is buried behind the church.

Nearby, the famous South Carolina poet, Henry Timrod is buried. The rough stone boulder marking his grave and the iron fence around the lot were placed there by the "Timrod Society" some years ago (1901). It was said there was nothing to mark his resting place. However, that was a mistake, as a graceful little marble shaft had been erected by his friends, among them the Prestons and Hamptons.

One interesting grave is that of an old and faithful sexton of the church, Pleasant Good. He served the church many years and his grave is near the corner of the yard on the Gervais Street side.

Attorney General Leroy F. Youmans, Chancellor James P. Carroll, Hon. Joseph Daniel Pope, are lawyers of note buried in the beautiful yard among a host of others who have served church, city and state.

Mention must be made of the live-oak tree on the south side of the church planted by Dr. Evans and General Hampton. The tree came from the General's old home place, "Millwood." On the same side of the church, near Senate Street, is a smaller oak which Dr. Phillips, M. C. Heath and Miss Carrie Berry planted on March 26, 1926.

The Churchyard chapter of the Daughters of the Holy Cross sees to the care of the cemetery. Provision has been made in certain wills and otherwise for the upkeep of family lots, and some funds are included in the parish budget for the church-yard. It is, however, largely through the personal service of women of the parish that the churchyard has been kept a fitting resting place for the beloved and honored dead of the parish.

A visitor to Columbia in the spring of 1937 came often to this quiet space set within the busy city's noise and stir, and of these visits wrote this line, describing well this God's-acre in the shadow of the church:

"I have found a beautiful spot, Trinity Episcopal Churchyard, one of the most beautiful places in Columbia. A world of peace and love that knows no hatred, turmoil or strife, where one is at peace with God and the world."

WARDENS AND VESTRYMEN

There appears to be no complete record or minutes of the congregational meetings of Trinity Church prior to 1883.

It has been impossible to ascertain who constituted the members of the vestry prior to that time except for the year 1875.

Below appear the names of the wardens and vestrymen:

1875

WARDENS	VESTRYMEN
Alex R. Taylor	Jno. B. Palmer
R. W. Gibbes, M. D.	E. W. Seibels
	Wm. Wallace
	Hugh S. Thompson
	E. H. Heinitsh
	W. R. Cathcart
	John E. Gyles

1883

A. R. Taylor	Gov. H. S. Thompson
William Wallace	Thomas Taylor
	John C. Haskell
	George S. Trezevant
	W. H. Gibbes
	C. F. Hampton
	C. J. Iredell

1884

A. R. Taylor	Gov. H. S. Thompson
William Wallace	W. H. Gibbes
	Thomas Taylor
	M. T. Bartlett
	C. J. Iredell
	John C. Haskell
	C. F. Hampton

1885

C. F. Hampton	W. H. Gibbes
E. W. Seibels	Thomas Taylor

Wardens	Vestrymen
	M. T. Bartlett
	John C. Haskell
	John Taylor
	W. E. Stoney

1886

E. W. Seibels	Thomas Taylor
W. H. Gibbes	W. E. Stoney
	Gov. H. S. Thompson
	John Taylor
	J. B. Ezell
	R. S. DesPortes
	M. T. Bartlett

1887

E. W. Seibels	R. W. Shand
W. H. Gibbes	W. E. Stoney
	M. T. Bartlett
	John Taylor
	Dr. B. W. Taylor
	J. B. Ezell
	R. S. DesPortes

1888

W. H. Gibbes	John Taylor
Robert W. Shand	Dr. B. W. Taylor
	M. T. Bartlett
	Dr. A. N. Talley
	John T. Sloan, Jr.
	J. B. Ezell
	W. B. Stanley

1889

W. H. Gibbes	Dr. A. N. Talley
Robert W. Shand	John T. Sloan, Jr.
	J. B. Ezell
	Dr. B. W. Taylor

WARDENS	VESTRYMEN
	R. S. DesPortes
	John Taylor
	M. T. Bartlett

1890

W. H. Gibbes	Dr. A. N. Talley
Robert W. Shand	John T. Sloan, Jr.
	J. B. Ezell
	Dr. B. W. Taylor
	R. S. DesPortes
	John Taylor
	M. T. Bartlett

1891

W. H. Gibbes	John Taylor
Robert W. Shand	Dr. A. N. Talley
	John T. Sloan, Jr.
	R. S. DesPortes
	J. B. Ezell
	Dr. B. W. Taylor
	M. T. Bartlett

1892

W. H. Gibbes	John Taylor
Robert W. Shand	Dr. A. N. Talley
	John T. Sloan, Jr.
	R. S. DesPortes
	J. B. Ezell
	Dr. B. W. Taylor
	M. T. Bartlett

1893

W. H. Gibbes	Dr. B. W. Taylor
Robert W. Shand	John Taylor
	Dr. A. N. Talley
	R. S. DesPortes
	J. B. Ezell
	John T. Sloan, Jr.
	John P. Thomas, Jr.

1894

Wardens	Vestrymen
W. H. Gibbes	Dr. B. W. Taylor
Robert W. Shand	Dr. A. N. Talley
	J. B. Ezell
	John Taylor
	R. S. DesPortes
	John T. Sloan
	John P. Thomas, Jr.

1895

W. H. Gibbes	Dr. B. W. Taylor
Robert W. Shand	Dr. A. N. Talley
	John Taylor
	R. S Desportes
	John T. Sloan
	J. B. Ezell
	John P. Thomas, Jr.

1896

R. W. Shand	Dr. A. N. Talley
W. H. Gibbes	Dr. B. W. Taylor
	John T. Sloan
	John Taylor
	J. B. Ezell
	R. S. DesPortes
	John P. Thomas, Jr.

1897

R. W. Shand	Dr. B. W. Taylor (resigned)
Dr. A. N. Talley	R. S. DesPortes
(died) succeeded by	J. H. Walker
Dr. B. W. Taylor	Geo. L. Baker
	John T. Seibels
	John P. Thomas, Jr.
	Wilie Jones
	John Taylor

1898

WARDENS	VESTRYMEN
R. W. Shand	John Taylor
Dr. B. W. Taylor	Allen Jones
	J. H. Walker
	Geo. L. Baker
	John T. Seibels
	John P. Thomas, Jr.
	Wilie Jones

1899

Robert W. Shand	Geo. L. Baker
Dr. B. W. Taylor	Allen Jones
	Wilie Jones
	John T. Seibels
	John Taylor
	John P. Thomas, Jr.
	Julius H. Walker

1900

Robert W. Shand	John Taylor
Dr. B. W. Taylor	John P. Thomas, Jr.
	Wilie Jones
	Allen Jones
	Julius H. Walker
	Geo. L. Baker
	John T. Seibels

1901

Robert W. Shand	John Taylor
Dr. B. W. Taylor	John P. Thomas, Jr.
	Wilie Jones
	Allen Jones
	Julius H. Walker
	Geo. L. Baker
	John T. Seibels

1902

WARDENS	VESTRYMEN
Robert W. Shand	John Taylor
Dr. B. W. Taylor	John P. Thomas, Jr.
	Wilie Jones
	Allen Jones
	Julius H. Walker
	George L. Baker
	John T. Seibels

1903

Robert W. Shand	John P. Thomas, Jr.
Dr. B. W. Taylor	John T. Seibels
	Geo. L. Baker
	Wilie Jones
	Judge A. C. Haskell
	Julius H. Walker
	John Taylor

1904

Robert W. Shand	John Taylor
Dr. B. W. Taylor	Julius H. Walker
	Wilie Jones
	Geo. L. Baker
	John T. Seibels
	Dr. Theo. M. DuBose
	Halcott P. Green

1905

Robert W. Shand	Wilie Jones
Dr. B. W. Taylor	John T. Seibels
	J. H. Walker
	Geo. L. Baker
	H. P. Green
	Dr. T. M. DuBose
	G. A. Guignard

1906

WARDENS	VESTRYMEN
Allen Jones	T. H. Gibbes
John T. Seibels	G. A. Guignard
	Dr. T. M. DuBose
	G. E. Shand
	H. P. Green
	A. S. Gaillard
	John Taylor

1907

Allen Jones	J. M. Bell
John T. Seibels	Dr. T. M. DuBose
	T. H. Gibbes
	Wilie Jones
	Dr. A. B. Knowlton
	B. W. Ravenel
	Dr. William Weston

1908

Allen Jones	T. H. Gibbes
R. W. Shand	J. M. Bell
	Dr. Wm. Weston
	A. S. Gaillard
	Dr. A. B. Knowlton
	G. E. Shand
	G. A. Guignard

1909

Allen Jones	T. H. Gibbes
Robert W. Shand	J. M. Bell
	Dr. Wm. Weston
	A. S. Gaillard
	Dr. A. B. Knowlton
	G. E. Shand
	G. A. Guignard

1910

WARDENS	VESTRYMEN
Allen Jones	G. A. Guignard
Robert W. Shand	Robert Moorman
	John T. Seibels
	T. H. Gibbes
	D. C. Ray
	George L. Baker
	George G. Moseley

1911

Allen Jones	G. A. Guignard
Robert W. Shand	G. L. Baker
	D. C. Ray
	George G. Moseley
	Robert Moorman
	John T. Seibels
	W. M. Shannon

1912

Allen Jones	G. L. Baker
Robert W. Shand	G. A. Guignard
	George G. Moseley
	Robert Moorman
	D. C. Ray
	W. M. Shannon
	John T. Seibels

1913

Robert W. Shand	O. F. Hart
John T. Seibels	Robert Moorman
	W. M. Shannon
	A. S. Gaillard
	G. A. Guignard
	D. C. Ray
	George L. Baker

1914

WARDENS	VESTRYMEN
Robert W. Shand	Robert Moorman
John T. Seibels	W. A. Clarkson
	G. A. Guignard
	O. F. Hart
	W. M. Shannon
	A. S. Gaillard
	George L. Baker

1915

John T. Seibels	Robert Moorman
George L. Baker	J. Nelson Frierson
(resigned) succeeded by	O. F. Hart
G. A. Guignard	G. A. Guignard (resigned)
	J. S. Middleton
	W. A. Clarkson
	Carroll H. Jones
	George L. Baker

1916

John T. Seibels	Robert Moorman
G. A. Guignard	James H. Fowles
	Wm. M. Shand
	W. W. Ball
	J. N. Frierson
	Dr. J. H. Taylor
	W. M. Shannon

1917

John T. Seibels	W. M. Shannon
G. A. Guignard	Wm. M. Shand
	James H. Fowles
	Dr. J. H. Taylor
	W. W. Ball
	Dr. LaBruce Ward
	L. P. Chamberlayne

1918

WARDENS	VESTRYMEN
John T. Seibels	S. T. Sparkman
G. A. Guignard	J. N. Frierson
	W. S. Nelson
	J. W. St. John
	Robert Moorman
	Jos. M. Bell
	Carroll H. Jones

1919

John T. Seibels	Wm. M. Shand
G. A. Guignard	W. S. Nelson
	Carroll H. Jones
	W. M. Shannon
	S. T. Sparkman
	John D. Bell
	Robert Moorman

1920

John T. Seibels	Gustaf Sylvan
G. A. Guignard	R. E. Carwile
	W. M. Shannon
	Wm. M. Shand
	J. D. Bell
	David G. Ellison
	W. T. Green

1921

John T. Seibels	Gustaf Sylvan
G. A. Guignard	Christie Benet
	D. G. Ellison
	R. E. Carwile
	Walter T. Green
	George C. Taylor
	A. McI. Griffin

1922

WARDENS	VESTRYMEN
John T. Seibels	Christie Benet
G. A. Guignard	A. McI. Griffin
	Frank H. Gibbes
	E. F. Lucas
	J. B. Murphy
	George L. Baker
	Dr. N. B. Heyward

1923

John T. Seibels	George L. Baker
G. A. Guignard	Dr. N. B. Heyward
	James B. Murphy
	Wm. M. Shand
	Dr. T. M. DuBose
	W. Bedford Moore, Jr.
	Frank T. Parker

1924

John T. Seibels	W. M. Shand
G. A. Guignard	Dr. T. M. DuBose, Sr.
	A. McI. Griffin
	W. M. Manning
	W. M. Shannon
	W. S. Nelson
	W. B. Moore, Jr.

1925

John T. Seibels	Wm. S. Nelson
G. A. Guignard	A. McI. Griffin
	W. M. Manning
	W. M. Shannon
	Dr. T. M. DuBose, Sr.
	Landon C. Jones
	H. J. Gregg

1926

Wardens	Vestrymen
Dr. T. M. DuBose, Sr.	John T. Seibels
R. I. Manning	G. A. Guignard
	H. J. Gregg
	Landon C. Jones
	E. L. Wingfield
	J. M. Bell
	M. C. Heath

1927

Dr. T. M. DuBose, Sr.	John T. Seibels
R. I. Manning	H. J. Gregg
	E. L. Wingfield
	J. M. Bell
	M. C. Heath
	R. B. Sloan
	M. B. Hutchinson

1928

Dr. T. M. DuBose, Sr.	R. I. Manning
W. M. Shand	Robert Moorman, Sr.
	H. Gordon Kenna
	M. B. Hutchinson
	R. B. Sloan
	J. B. Urquhart
	Frank J. Dana

NOTE: John T. Seibels was made an honorary life member of the Vestry.

1929

Dr. T. M. DuBose, Sr.	R. I. Manning
W. M. Shand	Robert Moorman, Sr.
	Frank J. Dana
	D. C. Heyward
	W. S. Nelson
	D. G. Ellison
	James B. Urquhart

1930

WARDENS	VESTRYMEN
R. I. Manning	D. C. Heyward
W. M. Shand	D. G. Ellison
	W. S. Nelson
	Dr. T. M. DuBose, Sr.
	Malcolm Miller
	W. J. Keenan
	M. C. Heath

1931

Dr. T. M. DuBose, Sr.	M. C. Heath
W. M. Shand	Malcolm Miller
	W. J. Keenan
	M. C. Lumpkin
	O. Lee Gordon
	E. L. Wingfield
	G. H. Crawford

NOTE: Gov. R. I. Manning was elected honorary life member of the Vestry.

1932

Dr. T. M. DuBose, Sr.	G. H. Crawford
Robert Moorman, Sr.	O. Lee Gordon
	M. C. Lumpkin
	E. L. Wingfield
	Christie Benet
	C. H. Jones
	Dr. N. B. Heyward

1933

Dr. T. M. DuBose, Sr.	Christie Benet
Robert Moorman, Sr.	Dr. N. B. Heyward
	C. H. Jones
	John A. Chase
	B. W. Ravenel
	John J. Seibels
	George E. LaFaye

1934

WARDENS	VESTRYMEN
Dr. T. M. DuBose, Sr.	John A. Chase
Robert Moorman, Sr.	George E. LaFaye
	B. W. Ravenel
	John J. Seibels
	Wm. E. Gonzales
	W. J. Keenan
	Dr. Wm. Weston, Jr.

1935

Robert Moorman, Sr.	W. J. Keenan
Wm. E. Gonzales	Dr. Wm. Weston, Jr.
	Christie Benet
	G. H. Crawford
	R. E. Carwile
	C. H. Jones
	C. M. Schmidt

NOTE: Dr. T. M. DuBose, Sr., was made an honorary life member of the Vestry.

1936

Wm. E. Gonzales	Christie Benet
Carroll H. Jones	G. H. Crawford
	C. M. Schmidt
	John T. Sloan
	Clark D. Waring
	Cosmo L. Walker
	A. R. Goodwyn, Jr.

1937

Wm. E. Gonzales	Alfred R. Goodwyn, Jr.
Carroll H. Jones	David S. DuBose
	Kirkman Finlay
	W. Dixon Foster
	John T. Sloan
	Cosmo L. Walker
	Clark D. Waring
	Dr. Wm. Weston, Jr.

COMMUNICANTS OF TRINITY CHURCH, 1937

A

Abdalla, Marie Suzanne (Mrs. Elias)
Adams, Annie Shand (Mrs. C. L.)
Adams, Anne Shand
Adams, Charles Leverett
Adams, Lila
Albert, Janie Sabbagha (Mrs. Joseph)
Albert, Julia David (Mrs. David)
Albert, Joseph
Aldrich, Harriot
Aldrich, Roberta
Alexander, Edward George
Alexander, Evelyn Mary
Alexander, George
Alexander, Melvena (Mrs. E. G.)
Allen, Sallie Tobin (Mrs. A. T.)
Allison, Frances Huger
Allison, James Richard
Allison, Lanier Montgomery
Allison, Minnie Williamson (Mrs. E. L.)
Allison, Susy FitzSimons (Mrs. J. R.)
Allison, William Elmer
Allston, Mary Louise
Alston, William Algernon
Anderson, John Maxwell
Anderson, Sallie Blanding
Anderson, Willie Louise (Mrs. J. M.)
Andrews, Annie McKay (Mrs. M. H.)
Asbill, David St. Pierre
Asbill, Eleanor Hart (Mrs. H. W.)
Asbill, Pauline Porter (Mrs. D. S.)
Ashe, Edward Cohen
Ashe, Josephine Harriss (Mrs. E. C.)
Ashe, Margaret Devereux
Athans, Tamma Sabbagha (Mrs. Chris)
Atkinson, Lucy Mary (Mrs. J. M.)
Averill, Mary Margaret (Mrs. J. H.)
Ayoub, Alexander
Ayoub, Julia Ann Lyons (Mrs. E. J.)

Babcock, Mary B. Heyward (Mrs. Wm. S.)
Bailey, Henrietta Geddes
Baker, Harriet Kershaw Lang (Mrs. L. T.)
Baker, Leonard Theodore
Baker, Stephan Ross
Baldwin, Esther Lillian
Baldwin, George
Baldwin, Kenneth William
Baldwin, Minnie Elizabeth (Mrs. Geo.)
Baldwin, Sue Kennedy (Mrs. K. W.)
Ball, Marjorie Buhler (Mrs. R. W.)
Ball, Mary Venable
Ball, Mary Venable Minor (Mrs. T. F.)
Ball, Robert Wilson
Ball, Thomas Fauntleroy
Barkoot, Marie Magdeline (Mrs. S. N.)
Barkoot, Shahady N.
Barkoot, Mitchell
Barringer, Lawrence Scott
Barringer, Louise Dublin (Mrs. L. S.)
Barnes, Elizabeth Eldridge (Mrs. A. D.)
Barnwell, Mary Taylor (Mrs. W. M.)
Barron, Charles Henry
Barron, Eliza Singleton (Mrs. C. H., Sr.)
Barron, Mary Lowndes
Barron, Nancy Harrison (Mrs. C. H.)
Bashara, Adeeb
Bateman, Edith Courtenay (Mrs. J. M.)
Bateman, Edith Courtenay
Bateman, Labernia Lorick (Mrs. W. C.)
Bateman, William Courtenay
Beattie, Daisy Hayne (Mrs. H. C.)
Beckham, Virginia Amanda (Mrs. W. K.)
Beckham, William Kinsler
Bell, Blanche Inman

Bell, Helen Gayle
Bell, Helen Iredell
Bell, Helen Jones (Mrs. J. M.)
Bell, Henrietta Brantley (Mrs. John)
Bell, John
Bell, John DuPont
Bell, John DuPont, Jr.
Bell, Joseph Milligan
Bell, Maria Locke (Mrs. J. D.)
Bell, Theodore Augustus, Jr.
Belser, Anne Gordon
Belser, Catherine Bayard
Belser, Clinch Heyward
Belser, Harriet Haynsworth
Belser, Irvine Furman
Belser, Irvine Furman, Jr.
Belser, Margaret Campbell
Belser, Mary Heyward (Mrs. I. F.)
Belser, Mary Heyward
Belser, William Gordon
Benet, Alice Van Yeveren Haskell (Mrs. C.)
Benet, Alice Van Yeveren
Benet, Christie
Benton, Ellen Legare Townsend (Mrs. W. S.)
Benton, William Spann
Berry, Katherine Elizabeth
Berry, Katherine Fickling (Mrs. G. M.)
Best, Effie (Mrs. E. J.)
Bishop, Homer Gould
Black, Donal
Black, Fannie Rose (Mrs. J. M.)
Black, James Menzies, Jr.
Black, Theodore Hayne
Blackwell, William Maud Riser (Mrs. E. A.)
Bollin, Alexander Wright
Bollin, John Hodge
Bollin, Lillian Wright
Bollin, Mary Bruton (Mrs. J. H.)
Bollin, Mary Bruton
Bonn, Ewing Tucker
Bookter, Kate Yates (Mrs. W. P.)
Bookter, William Preston, Jr.
Bostick, Lucy Hampton (Mrs. H.)
Boyd, Frances Boykin (Mrs. W. C.)

Boyd, Mary Keller (Mrs. Wm. A.)
Boyd, Mary Keller
Boyd, William Augustus
Boyd, William Clarence, Jr.
Boyle, Margaret Anne McGregor
Boyle, Margaret McGregor (Mrs. T. B.)
Boyle, Thomas Belton
Brabham, Lucile Kingman (Mrs. H. J., Jr.)
Brabham, Marion Roberta Sample (Mrs. H. J.)
Bradham, Randolph
Bradley, Jane Trenholm (Mrs. F. W.)
Bradley, Jane Vanderhorst Heyward
Brenchley, Katherine Watson (Mrs. G. A.)
Briggs, Virginia Carter
Brooker, Beecher Owens
Brooker, Frances Elizabeth
Brooker, Julia Daniel (Mrs. B. O., Sr.)
Brooks, Elizabeth Bell (Mrs. M. B.)
Brooks, Jane Adams
Brooks, John Hampden
Brooks, Linnie LaBorde (Mrs. U. R.)
Brooks, Margaret
Brown, Anna Ramelle Sims (Mrs. T. C.)
Brown, DeLacy Brown
Brown, Ellamae Hood (Mrs. J. L.)
Brown, Elizabeth Tramwell Barnes (Mrs. E. E.)
Brown, Grace (Mrs. W. S.)
Brown, Joseph Lockwood
Brown, Reida Brown (Mrs. A. P.)
Brown, William Samuel
Bruorton, Enid Lucas Josey (Mrs. W. J.)
Bryan, Williams McIver, Jr.
Buchanan, Clara Hammond (Mrs. G. A., Jr.)
Burch, Charlotte Ellene
Burch, Ella Givan (Mrs. B. S.)
Burney, Floride Cunningham (Mrs. W. M.)

Butler, Ellen Iredell
Butler, Lillian Jones (Mrs. F. W. P.)

C

Cain, William Lowndes
Cain, Harriet Horry (Mrs. E. H.)
Cain, Isabel Lindsay (Mrs. J. R.)
Cain, James Ravenel
Cain, Pinckney Lowndes
Cain, William Lowndes
Cannon, Lizzie Nell McLellan (Mrs. T. E.)
Cannon, Thomas Evans
Cantey, Dorothy Hagood (Mrs. J. M., Jr.)
Cantey, Edward Brevard
Cantey, Edward Brevard, Jr.
Cantey, Elizabeth Childs (Mrs. J. M.)
Cantey, Evelyn Robertson
Cantey, Helen Robertson (Mrs. E. B.)
Cantey, Helen Robertson
Cantey, James Willis
Cantey, John Manning
Cantey, William Childs
Capers, Helen DuBose (Mrs. M.)
Carpenter, Edward Preston
Carpenter, Winnie Davis (Mrs. E. P.)
Carr, Hugh
Carr, Louise Marion
Carr, Mary Elizabeth
Carter, Anne Bohannan (Mrs. S. B.)
Carter, Kate Goode
Carter, Samuel Booker
Carwile, Richard Eugene
Cary, Edward Richard
Cary, Mary Lyman (Mrs. E. R.)
Cary, Jennie Green (Mrs. J. G.)
Cathcart, Annie Sloan (Mrs. J. A.)
Cathcart, Anne Sloan
Cathcart, Charles Dwight
Cathcart, Coles Heyward (Mrs. C. D.)
Cathcart, James Armstrong

Cathcart, John Sloan
Cathcart, Katherine Stewart
Cathcart, Louise Dwight (Mrs. E. C., Sr.)
Cato, Edgar Thomas
Cato, Elizabeth Keenan (Mrs. E. T.)
Caughman, Mamie Alice
Chase, John Alexander
Chase, Mary Wingfield (Mrs. J. A.)
Childs, Frances Sams (Mrs. R. G.)
Childs, Frances Sams
Childs, Robert Gibbes
Clark, Marietta Cathcart (Mrs. G. W.)
Clarke, Alice Urquhart (Mrs. R. R.)
Clarke, Burwell Boykin
Clarke, Rosa Heyward (Mrs. B. B.)
Clarke, Rufus Rivers
Clarkson, Allen Boykin
Clarkson, Nathaniel Heyward
Clarkson, Nathaniel Heyward, Jr.
Clews, Helen M. Kohler (Mrs. W. H.)
Clews, William Horace
Coker, Flora Wylie (Mrs. E. C.)
Coleman, James Bruce
Coles, Helen (Mrs. Stricker)
Conard, Aline Rucker (Mrs. R. A.)
Conard, Aline Russell
Conard, Joan
Conard, Robert Allen
Conard, Robert Allen, Jr.
Conder, Emma Mason (Mrs. J. W.)
Conder, Mary Helen
Cooper, Aurelia Elizabeth
Cooper, Claude Dock
Cooper, Eunice Stokes (Mrs. T. B.)
Cooper, Frances Kathryn (Mrs. G. F., Jr.)
Cooper, John Hankins, Jr.
Cooper, Margaret Harris (Mrs. P. A.)
Cooper, Mary Marjorie
Cooper, Paul Anderson
Cooper, Thomas Berry
Courtenay, Margaret Beattie (Mrs. St. J.)
Courtenay, Margaret Hayne Beattie

Cox, Elise Legare (Mrs. R. B.)
Cox, Radford Brantley
Craig, Emma Frierson (Mrs. E. L.)
Craighill, Mary Hamilton Haile
    (Mrs. A. L.)
Craps, John Ellis
Crary, Emmala Bacon Livingston
    (Mrs. W. A., Jr.)
Crary, William Alexander, Jr.
Crawford, Agnes Dilmore
Crawford, Agnes Pauline (Mrs. An-
    drew)
Crawford, Andrew
Crawford, Dorothy Vernon
Crawford, Geddings Hardy
Crawford, Jessie Thompson (Mrs.
    G. H.)
Crawford, John Alexander
Crawford, John Alexander, Jr.
Crawford, Lilah Hall (Mrs. An-
    drew, Sr.)
Crowson, Evelyn Caudle (Mrs. W.
    J.)
Crowson, William James
Cunningham, Sarah Ellen
Cunningham, Stella May
Curren, Grace Grindley (Mrs. W.
    F., Jr.)
Curren, William Francis, Jr.

Dana, Anne Simons
Dana, Francis Johnston
Dana, Francis Johnston, Jr.
Dana, Jane Tucker Fisher (Mrs. F.
    J.)
Dana, Mary Fisher
Darby, Lize
Darby, Sarah Adams (Mrs. Pres-
    ton)
Darby, Sarah Moore
Davis, Blanche O'Neale (Mrs. G.
    W., Sr.)
Davis, Edith Albert (Mrs. G. E. R.)
Davis, George E. R.
Davis, John McMahan
Davis, George Wilmot
Dehon, Helen Purdy (Mrs. Theo.
    Jr.)

Dehon, Theodore, Jr.
DeLoach, Mary Kershaw Blackwell
    (Mrs. S. D.)
DeLoach, Sirre Dubarque
Denny, Edward Riddle
Denny, Edward Riddle, Jr.
DePass, Addison Rutledge
DesPortes, Richard Smallwood
Detyens, Margaret Selby (Mrs. M.
    S.)
Dial, Bena Inglesby (Mrs. Geo. L.)
Dial, Charles Inglesby
Dial, George Louis
Dial, George Louis, Jr.
Dial, Dorothy Geer (Mrs. C. I.)
Dial, Mary Boyleston (Mrs. T. F.)
Dial, Thomas Frasier
Dial, Thomas Frasier, Jr.
Dick, George Lee
Dick, Minnie Coffin (Mrs. G. L.)
Dorn, Henry Hartzog
Dowe, Mamie Spann (Mrs. J. E.)
Doughty, Heloise Gibbes (Mrs. R.
    G.)
Doughty, Roger Gamble
Drew, Martha Yates (Mrs. W. D.)
Drew, William Dewitt
DuBose, Arianna Livingston (Mrs.
    D. S.)
DuBose, Beverley Means (Mrs. T.
    M.)
DuBose, David St. Pierre
DuBose, Hugh Hammond
DuBose, John Bratton
DuBose, John Bratton, Jr.
DuBose, Kitty Rion (Mrs. J. B.)
DuBose, Sarah Hammond (Mrs.
    T. M., Jr.)
DuBose, Theodore Marion
DuBose, Theodore Marion, Jr.
DuBose, Theodore Marion, III
DuBose, Virginia Carroll (Mrs. W.
    P.)
DuBose, William Porcher
Dunlap, Anne Beverley Jones (Mrs.
    B. B.)
Durden, Dessie Brown
Durden, Eva Belle Legare (Mrs. D.
    B.)

Dutrow, Ray H.
Dutrow, Ray H., Jr.
Dwight, Sidney Jamison

E

Earle, Henrietta (Mrs. Robt.)
Edens, Jane Gibbes (Mrs. H. H.)
Edmunds, Guerry Green (Mrs. Lamar)
Elliott, Daisy Barnwell King (Mrs. Wm., Jr.
Elliott, Leila Sams (Mrs. Wm.)
Elliott, Mildred Gibbes (Mrs. Talley)
Elliott, Sallie Stamps (Mrs. Wm., Sr.)
Elliott, Stephen
Elliott, William
Elliott, William, Jr.
Ellison, Cornelia Jackson (Mrs. D. G., Jr.)
Ellison, David Gaillard
Ellison, David Gaillard, Jr.
Ellison, James Hagood
Ellison, Robert Emmett
Ellison, Sophie Aldrich (Mrs. D. G.)
Ellison, Sophie Aldrich
Emmanuel, Sarah Jane Ward (Mrs. Nat.)
Espedahl, Elizabeth Stark (Mrs. K. S.)
Espedahl, Kaare S.
Evans, Mary Goodwyn (Mrs. Marion)

F

Fair, Celina Moore (Mrs. H. W.)
Fair, Henry Wilson
Fair, Herndon Moore
Fair, James Henry
Fair, Ray Taylor (Mrs. J. H.)
Farber, Elsie (Mrs. W. C.)
Farber, William Charles
Farr, Edwin Francis
Farr, James Starling, Jr.
Farr, Margaret McCreight (Mrs. E. F.)

Farr, Mary Grace McLendon (Mrs. J. S., Jr.)
Fellers, Anna LaBorde (Mrs. R. G.)
Fellers, Rufus Gustavus, Jr.
Ferrell, Clyde Miser
Ferrell, Martha (Mrs. C. M.)
Fielding, Emma Bronaugh
Finegan, Mary Southworth (Mrs. W. R.)
Finegan, William Robert
Finlay, Catherine McCarrell (Mrs. K.)
Finlay, Edward Reed
Finlay, Elinor Murray
Finlay, Kate Alice
Finlay, Kirkman George
Finlay, Kirkman
Finlay, Lucy Reed (Mrs. K. G.)
Finlay, Marian Ponsonby
Fisher, Mary Stoney (Mrs. T. H.)
Fitch, Alice Tiedeman (Mrs. F. B.)
Fitch, Alice
Fitch, Francis Burt
Fitch, Francis Burt, Jr.
Fitch, Mary Tiedeman
FitzSimons, Christopher
FitzSimons, Christopher, Jr.
FitzSimons, Frances Huger (Mrs. C., Sr.)
FitzSimons, Nathalie Heyward (Mrs. C.)
FitzSimons, Nathalie Heyward
Folline, Allen Gantt
Folline, Mary Deas Read (Mrs. A. G.)
Forbes, Mary Reynolds (Mrs. H. L.)
Forbes, Susan Reynolds
Ford, Charles LaHue
Ford, Elizabeth Henrietta
Ford, Mattie Deveaux
Foster, Harold Q.
Foster, Katherine Elizabeth (Mrs. W. D.)
Foster, William Dixon
Fouche, Heyward Hutchison
Fowles, Amelia Clarkson
Fowles, James Henry
Fowles, James Henry, Jr.

Fowles, Ruth Wellman (Mrs. J. H., Jr.

Fowles, Sophie Clarkson (Mrs. J. H.)

Fraser, Madeline

Free, Maude Oakman (Mrs. L. R.)

Frierson, James Nelson

Frierson, Louise Mazyck (Mrs. J. N.)

Fripp, Carolina Redwine (Mrs. R. A. L.)

Fripp, Robert Adam Lindley

Furtick, Daisy Cannon (Mrs. W. F.)

Furtick, William Fulton

G

Gaillard, Alfred Secundus

Gaillard, Alfred Secundus, Jr.

Gaillard, Christine Acree (Mrs. R. O.)

Gaillard, Julia Pickens (Mrs. W. F.)

Gaillard, Mabel O'Neale (Mrs. A. S.)

Gaillard, Richard O'Neale

Garner, Anne (Mrs. A.)

Gary, Frank Boyd

Gary, Maria Lee Evans (Mrs. F. B., Sr.)

Garzouzi, Elias

Gaston, Barbara Kathryn

Gause, Patience Shand (Mrs. Benj.)

Gibbes, Alexander Mason

Gibbes, Caroline LeConte (Mrs. A. M., Sr.)

Gibbes, Eugenia Salley (Mrs. J. H.)

Gibbes, Eugenia Salley

Gibbes, Frank Huger

Gibbes, Frank Huger, Jr.

Gibbes, Hunter Allston

Gibbes, Minnie Moore (Mrs. W. M.)

Gibbes, Susan Heyward

Gibbes, Susan Ravenel (Mrs. F. H.)

Gibbes, Viola Johnson (Mrs. H. A.)

Gibbes, William Moultrie

Glover, Elizabeth Kent

Glover, Gordon Logan (Mrs. Jos.)

Glover, Joseph

Gonzales, William Elliott (deceased)

Goodwyn, Alfred Raoul

Goodwyn, Alfred Raoul, Jr.

Goodwyn, Ellen Adela

Goodwyn, Lettie May (Mrs. A. R.)

Goodwyn, Mary Gaillard (Mrs. A. R., Jr.)

Gordon, Harriet Mehrtens (Mrs. O. L.)

Gordon, Oscar Lee (deceased)

Gordon, Oscar Lee, Jr.

Graham, Florence Denny (Mrs. F. A.)

Graham, Mary Lees

Graves, Margaruite Bryant

Graydon, Augustus Tompkins

Graydon, Clinton Tompkins

Graydon, Margaret Wallace

Graydon, Raven Simpkins (Mrs. C. T.)

Graydon, Sarah Lewis

Gregg, Harry Junius

Gregg, Harriet Hammond (Mrs. H. J.)

Gregory, Elizabeth Stanton (Mrs. E. S.)

Gregory, Harriet Holmes (Mrs. H. H.)

Grier, Frank Barron, Jr.

Grier, Helen Coles (Mrs. F. B., Jr.)

Griffin, Arthur McIver

Griffin, Emma Shannon (Mrs. A. McI.)

Griffin, Emily L'Artigue

Griffin, Emily Pinckney (Mrs. H. H.)

Griffin, Harry Hammond

Griffin, Katherine Pinckney

Griffin, Margaret Motte (Mrs. P. E.)

Griffin, Margaret Motte

Griffin, Peter Evans

Griffin, Peter Evans, Jr.

Guerard, Edward Percy

Guerry, Maryanne

Guignard, Caroline

Guignard, Christopher Gadsden

Guignard, Emilie Hill (Mrs. S. R., Sr.)

Guignard, Jane Bruce
Guignard, Mary
Guignard, Sanders Richardson
Guignard, Susan Richardson
Guignard, Susan McBryde (Mrs. C. G.)
Guignard, William Slann
Gulick, Laura
Gunter, Laura Perry (Mrs. L.)

H

Haile, Ella Cantey (Mrs. Benj.)
Hamby, Arthur Williams (deceased)
Hamby, Elizabeth McNulty (Mrs. A. W.)
Hamby, Lottie Derieux
Hamby, Mary Williams
Hamby, Theoditus Capers
Hammond, Blanche Orr (Mrs. A. H.)
Hammond, Hampton Bland
Hammond, Hampton Bland, Jr.
Hammond, James Henry
Hammond, Janie Marshall (Mrs. J. H.)
Hammond, Laura
Hammond, Minnie Bollin (Mrs. H. B.)
Hampton, Frank
Hampton, Harry Rutledge Elliott
Hampton, Mary Fleming (Mrs. F.)
Hane, Albert Elmore
Hane, Maisie Yates (Mrs. A. E.)
Hardy, Archibald
Hardy, Archibald, Jr.
Hardy, Elizabeth Cecil (Mrs. A.)
Hardy, Elizabeth Cecil
Hardy, Sarah Heyward (Mrs. A., Jr.)
Harris, Gabriella Feininger (Mrs. O. J.)
Hart, Elizabeth Trice (Mrs. W. A.)
Hart, Frances
Hart, George Childs
Hart, Nancy Childs (Mrs. O. F.)
Hart, Oliver Frank
Hart, Oliver James
Hart, William Augustus

Harth, Velda Frank Baxter (Mrs. W. H.)
Harth, William Henry
Harvin, Frank Madison, Jr.
Harvin, George Legare
Harvin, Leonie Druelle (Mrs. F. M.)
Harvin, Margaret Washington (Mrs. G. L.)
Hayne, Lillah Adams (Mrs. Theo B.) (deceased)
Hazlehurst, Valeria Brown (Mrs. W. Y.)
Heath, Elizabeth Tennent (Mrs. M. C.)
Heinitsh, Agnes Walker (Mrs. R. D.)
Heinitsh, Reginald Davis, Jr.
Henagan, Anne Rhodes
Henagan, Mary Gibson
Henning, Susanne Pope (Mrs. D.)
Henderson, Clara Stafford (Mrs. Rich.)
Henderson, Richard
Herbert, Georgia Hull (Mrs. R. B.)
Herbert, Georgia Hull
Herbert, James Hull
Herbert, Mary Baldwin
Herbert, Mildred Andrews (Mrs. W. C.)
Herbert, Robert Beverley
Herbert, Robert Beverley, Jr.
Herbert, William Columbus
Hester, Marie Azilee Brown (Mrs. E. O.)
Hester, Page Lane (Mrs. J. L., Jr.)
Heyward, Albert Rhett
Heyward, Alexander Campbell
Heyward, Beulah Hall (Mrs. A. C.)
Heyward, Caroline
Heyward, Dorothy Allen (Mrs. R. M.)
Heyward, Duncan Clinch
Heyward, Katherine Bayard
Heyward, Mariana Tabb (Mrs. B. H.)
Heyward, Mary Barksdale
Heyward, Nathaniel Barnwell

Heyward, Roger Moore
Heyward, Rosa Cantey (Mrs. A. R.)
Hines, Mary Sawyer Moore (Mrs. E. M.)
Hipp, Rebecca Stanton (Mrs. E. L.)
Hodges, Benjamin Deland (deceased)
Hodges, Elizabeth Henderson
Hodges, Virginia Childs Reynolds (Mrs. B. D.)
Hodges, Virginia Reynolds
Holmes, James Gadsden
Holmes, James Gadsden, Jr.
Holmes, Minnie Farmer (Mrs. J. G.)
Hood, Roberta Dismukes Wylly (Mrs. B.)
Hood, Robin
Hopkins, Jane McDowell (Mrs. T. J.)
Hopkins, Theodore Jervey
Hopson, Edith McMillan (Mrs. W. H.)
Hopson, William Herbert
Horne, Marion
Hughes, Elizabeth Mitchell (Mrs. E. M.)
Hughes, Adeline Harriette
Hunter, Caroline Gibbes
Hunter, Daisy McGregor (Mrs. J. E., Jr.)
Hunter, Ella deSaussure
Hunter, James Edwin, Jr.
Hutchinson, Katharine Huntington (Mrs. M. B.)
Hutchinson, Moultrie Brailsford
Hutchison, Charlotte Middleton (Mrs. W. G., Sr.)
Hutchison, Charlotte Haskell
Hutchison, Walter George
Hykil, Olga Helen
Hykil, Selma (Mrs. G. L.)

I

Inglesby, Susan Manning (Mrs. L.)
Irby, Helen Lightbourne
Irby, John Lyllian McFarlan

Irby, Marjorie Evans (Mrs. J. L. M.)
Irby, Sarah LeConte Davis (Mrs. S. A.)
Izard, Sallie Coles Heyward (Mrs. R. deL.)

J

James, Clara Tillman (Mrs. H. M.)
James, Hugh McCuthen
Jenkins, Mary Gambrill
Jennings, Florence Brown (Mrs. J. W.)
Jervey, Harold Edward
Jervey, Harold Edward, Jr.
Jervey, Stella White (Mrs. H. E.)
Jeter, Thomas Cofield
Johnson, Janet Henry (Mrs. J. C.)
Johnson, Mary Gale
Jones, Anne Iredell
Jones, Annie Caldwell (Mrs. Wilie)
Jones, Augusta Porcher (Mrs. Allen)
Jones, Caldwell
Jones, Carroll Hammett
Jones, Frances Ledbetter (Mrs. L. C.)
Jones, Grace McGill (Mrs. Iredell, Sr.)
Jones, Helen Leavenworth
Jones, Iredell
Jones, Landon Caldwell
Jones, Landon Caldwell, Jr.
Jones, Robert Ledbetter
Jones, Virginia Carroll (Mrs. C. H.)

K

Kaminer, Earle Manning
Kaminer, Mary Hull (Mrs. E. M.)
Kaminer, Mary Hull
Keenan, Elmira deGraffenreid (Mrs. W. J.)
Keenan, William Joseph
Keenan, William Joseph, Jr.
Keenan, Richard Charlton, Jr.
Kelly, Helen Prince (Mrs. W. T.)
Kelly, William Tolson

Kendall, Berrien Williams

Kendall, Edith Snodgrass (Mrs. B. W.)

Kendall, Francis Drake

Kendall, Louise Berrien (Mrs. F. D.)

Kenna, Elizabeth Sharon

Kenna, Henry Gordon

Kenna, Katherine Blount (Mrs. H. G.)

Kenna, Kathleen Blount

Kennett, Mary King (Mrs. S. C.)

Kennett, Samuel Corbett

Khouri, Marie Garzouzi (Mrs. M.)

Khouri, Sallie

King, Mary Lowndes (Mrs. A. E.)

Knowlton, Alice Wilson (Mrs. B. A.)

Knowlton, Benjamin Almy

Knowlton, Charles Wilson

Knowlton, Claudia Earle (Mrs. A. B.)

Knowlton, Claudia Earle

Kohn, Dorita Moise (Mrs. August)

L

LaBorde, Ada Carroll

LaBorde, Frances Hutto (Mrs. J. B.)

LaBorde, Jean Baptiste

Lafaye, Charlotte Lucas (Mrs. G. E.)

Lafaye, George Eugene

Lafaye, George Eugene, Jr.

Lafaye, Mary Doar

Lafaye, Marguerite Rayal

Lafaye, Nell Murray (Mrs. R. S.)

Lafaye, Robert Stoddard

Lafaye, William Lucas

Lamar, Elsie Nixon (Mrs. W. F.)

Lane, Richard Ivanhoe

Lane, Ruth Mayes (Mrs. R. I.)

Lane, Sarah Boyd

Lane, Thomas Wannamaker

Langley, Arthur Fernando

Langley, Claudia Seabrook (Mrs. A. F.)

L'Artigue, Emily

Lawrence, Catherine Gould (Mrs. L. D.)

Lawrence, Lloyd Dean

Lawrence, Patricia Dean

Leek, Gladys Hayes (Mrs. J. B.)

Leek, John Bannister

Legare, Isabel Robertson (Mrs. A. E.)

Lem, Frank

Leonard, Sarah Holland

Lever, Asbury Francis, Jr.

Lever, Lucile Scurry Butler (Mrs. A. F.)

Lever, Mary Catherine

Lewis, David Sloan

Lewis, David Sloan, Jr.

Lewis, John Earle

Lewis, Lucy Walton

Lewis, Reuben Walton (Mrs. D. S.)

Lide, Charlotte Brown

Lide, Marguerite Andrews (Mrs. R. E.)

Locke, Annie

Love, Katherine Tennent (Mrs. W. D.)

Lucas, Floride DePass (Mrs. T. C.)

Lumpkin, Alva Moore

Lumpkin, Alva Moore, Jr.

Lumpkin, Frances White (Mrs. M. C.)

Lumpkin, Hope Henry

Lumpkin, John Henderson

Lumpkin, Mary Isabel Henderson (Mrs. H. H., Sr.)

Lumpkin, Mary Waties

Lumpkin, Robert Lucas

Lumpkin, Sumter Thomas (Mrs. A. M.)

Lykes, Eleanor Bray

Lykes, Sarah Martin (Mrs. H. P.)

Lyles, Evelyn Robertson (Mrs. J. B. S.)

M

Mack, Lily (Mrs. George)

Mack, Nellie Tibshrany (Mrs. Jos.)

Magoffin, Kate Manning (Mrs. R.)

Manning, John Adger

Manning, Katherine Heath (Mrs. B. D.)

Manning, Lelia Meredith (Mrs. R. I.)

Manning, Margaret Elliott (Mrs. J. A.)

Marshall, Elizabeth Arnold

Marshall, Ella Walton Richardson (Mrs. Foster)

Marshall, Foster

Marshall, Helen Bruton (Mrs. J. Q.)

Marshall, James Quitman

Marshall, Mary C.

Martin, Charles Wallace

Martin, Kathryn Geer

Martin, Louise Keenan (Mrs. L. K.)

Matney, Addie May Mack (Mrs. M. A.)

Matney, Emma Evelyn

Matney, Mitry Abraham

Matthews, Ellie

Mayer, Nancy Phillips (Mrs. O. B.)

McCarty, Donald

McCarty, Mary Louise Hunter (Mrs. Don.)

McCaw, Genevieve Anderson (Mrs. W. H.)

McCaw, William Henry

McCaw, William Henry, Jr.

McCrady, Robert Lane

McCutcheon, Elizabeth Heyward (Mrs. G. T.)

McDowell, Jennie McAllister (Mrs. R. H.)

McGowan, William Campbell

McGregor, Daisy Wells (Mrs. E. C.)

McKay, Anne Lowndes

McKay, Anne Walker (Mrs. Douglas)

McKay, Douglas, Jr.

McKay, Julius Walker

McKenzie, Eugenie Paul Tillman (Mrs. J. R.)

McMaster, Alida Gonzales (Mrs. Richard)

Meares, Kate deRosset

Meetze, Bessie Lowe (Mrs. A. M.)

Melton, Henrietta Loeb (Mrs. W. D., Sr.)

Melton, Martha Tompkins (Mrs. J. T.)

Melton, William Davis

Metts, Walter Arthur

Mikell, Caroline Elizabeth

Mikell, Margaret Gaillard (Mrs. W. T.)

Mikell, MacFarland Herd

Mikell, Walter Taylor

Mikell, Walter Taylor, Jr.

Mikell, William Calhoun

Miller, Dorothy Walker

Miller, Eula Piver (Mrs. M. J.)

Miller, Eustace Percival, Jr.

Miller, Katherine Wylie

Miller, Malcolm Jerome

Miller, Nathalie Heyward (Mrs. C. W.)

Miller, Nell Darby (Mrs. E. P.)

Miller, William Wallace

Mimms, Earle Watson

Mimms, Edwin Herbert

Mimms, Hubert Leonard

Miot, Charles Henry

Miot, Janie Belle Heath (Mrs. C. H.)

Moore, Annie Lee Adicks

Moore, Austin Talley

Moore, Elizabeth Finley (Mrs. W. B., Jr.)

Moore, Elizabeth Finley

Moore, Joseph Henry

Moore, Kate Lorraine Crawford (Mrs. T. T.)

Moore, Mary Frances Walker (Mrs. A. T.)

Moore, Sarah Gist

Moore, Thomas Thompson

Moore, Walter Bedford, Jr.

Moore, Walter Bedford, III

Moorefield, Charles Henry

Moorefield, Ruth Watkins (Mrs. C. H., Sr.)

Moorman, Blanche Rowlette (Mrs. Robt., Jr.)

Moorman, Elizabeth Cotton (Mrs. Robt.)
Moorman, Joseph James
Moorman, Robert
Moorman, Robert, III
Morris, Minnie Jenkins (Mrs. W. L.)
Moseley, George Gretter
Moseley, Pauline (Mrs. G. G., Sr.)
Moseley, Stuart Everett (Mrs. G. G.)
Mullins, Constance
Mullins, Edward Wade
Mullins, Emily Price (Mrs. W. G.)
Mullins, Julia
Mullins, Katherine Clark (Mrs. E. W.)
Mullins, Walter Guerry
Mullins, Walter Guerry, Jr.
Mullins, William Price
Mullins, William Sidney
Murphy, Edith Sanborn (Mrs. S. J.)
Murphy, Edith Aldrich
Murphy, Elizabeth Sanborn
Murphy, James Bryson
Murphy, Katherine Zemp (Mrs. J. B.)
Murphy, Katherine deLoache
Murray, James George
Murray, James George, Jr.
Murray, Margaret English (Mrs. J. G.)
Murray, Norman Page
Murray, Sara Louise (Mrs. N. P.)

N

Nelson, Nina Geddes (Mrs. W. S.)
Nelson, Nina Geddes
Nelson, Patrick Henry
Nelson, Sarah Monrovia Watts (Mrs. S. M. W.)
Nelson, William Shannon
Norment, Frank Eugene
Norment, Martha Jennings (Mrs. F. E.)

O

Old, Charles Wesley
Oliver, Caldwell Hardy
Oliver, Eleanor McKinnon (Mrs. C. H.)
Olson, George Edgar
Olson, George Edgar, Jr.
Olson, Ida (Mrs. G. E.)
Otis, Barbara
Ott, Margaret Powers (Mrs. T. O.)
Owens, Clara Ellen Forbes (Mrs. C. E.)
Owens, Frank Capers
Owens, Ida Hand (Mrs. F. C.)
Owings, Alfred Berry, Jr.
Owings, Frederick Alfred Berry
Owings, Mary Olive Palmer (Mrs. A. B., Jr.)

P

Papajohn, Constantina (Mrs. Pete)
Parker, Caroline Cureton (Mrs. F. T.)
Parker, James Rose
Parker, Sally deSaussure (Mrs. J. R.)
Patterson, Clara Ellen Owens (Mrs. Eugene)
Pechilis, Mary (Mrs. Peter)
Pechilis, Peter
Pender, Shepherd Turner
Penney, James Theophilus
Perry, Leonilla
Peyton, George Vivien
Phillips, Ella Parr
Phillips, Ella Reese (Mrs. H. D.)
Phillips, Henry Disbrow
Phillips, Henrietta Desborough
Pinckney, Francis Morris
Pinckney, Caroline Walker (Mrs. F. M.)
Platte, Edna Grace Crapps (Mrs. L. L.)
Platte, Louis Leroy
Pope, Annie Byrd Miller (Mrs. J. W. R., Sr.)
Pope, John William Rippon

Pope, Sarah White (Mrs. J. W. R.)
Pope, Joseph Daniel
Powell, Catherine Piez (Mrs. J. D.)
Pringle, Ellen Elliott (Mrs. J. J.)
Prioleau, Alice Chisolm (Mrs. J. G.)
Prioleau, John Guerard

R

Ravenel, Bruce Walker
Ravenel, Bruce Walker, Jr.
Ravenel, James Middleton
Ravenel, Margaret Middleton (Mrs. B. W.)
Rawls, Mary Frances
Read, Eugene Stoney
Read, Robert Vaux
Reamer, Cornelia Youmans
Reamer, Cornelius Youmans
Reamer, Ida Salley (Mrs. C. Y.)
Reamer, Margaret Hamilton (Mrs. W. S.)
Reamer, William Shell
Redwine, Isaac Franklin
Redwine, Lillian Rowena
Redwine, Pearl Mobley (Mrs. I. F., Sr.)
Reed, Margaret Ravenel (Mrs. C. L.)
Reese, Aimee Urquhart (Mrs. J. T., Jr.)
Reese, Jesse Timothy, Jr.
Refo, Gertrude Harby (Mrs. G. H.)
Rembert, Allen Jones
Rembert, Catherine Phillips (Mrs. A. J.)
Reynolds, Emily Bellinger (Mrs. J. S.)
Reynolds, Joan Schreiner
Reynolds, Virginia Vanderhoof
Rhame, Lillian Herring (Mrs. S. C.)
Rhame, Lillian Herring
Rice, Emert Solon
Richardson, Henry Warren, Jr.
Richardson, Julia Courtenay (Mrs. H. B.)
Rion, Alva Holbrook
Roach, Eugene Johnson
Roach, Harriet Moss (Mrs. E. J.)

Robb, Alexander Wentworth
Robb, Margaret Heyward (Mrs. C. B.)
Robb, Nathaniel Heyward
Roberts, Hamilton Warren (Mrs. Carlisle)
Robertson, Elizabeth
Robertson, Lutie Durham
Robertson, Margaret
Robertson, Mary Gayle
Robertson, Mary Martin (Mrs. T. J.)
Robertson, Thomas James
Rogers, Edward Pou
Rogers, Emma King (Mrs. E. P.)
Roman, Charles Beauregard
Roman, Charles Beauregard, Jr.
Roman, Eleanor Van Benthuysen (Mrs. C. B.)
Rose, William Henry
Rowe, Walter
Rowe, Adeline (Mrs. Walter)
Rowlette, Beatrice (Mrs. W. G.)

S

Sabbagha, Caladice Gladys
Sabbagha, Effie (Mrs. S. A.)
Sabbagha, George
Sabbagha, Isabel Margaret
Sabbagha, Olga
Sabbagha, Philip Christmas
Sabbagha, Rosalie Anne
Sabbahga, Saleemie (Mrs. Geo.)
Sabbagha, Shickre Andrew
Sabbagha, Victoria Juliet
Salley, Harriet Milledge (Mrs. A. S.)
Salley, Joseph Daniel Pope
Salley, Mary Stoney (Mrs. A. P.) (deceased)
Salley, May Pickens
Salley, Reed Stoney
Salley, Rosalie Fleming (Mrs. R. S.)
Sams, Camilla Johnson (Mrs. S.)
Sams, Caroline Earle (Mrs. J. H., Sr.),
Sanders, Alexander Mulling

Sanders, Annie Gribbin (Mrs. W. J.)

Sanders, Henrietta Thomas (Mrs. A. M.)

Sands, Jerome Daly

Sands, Margaret Urquhart (Mrs. J. D.)

Sasnett, Mary Seabrook (Mrs. R. M., Jr.)

Sasnett, Richard Maxwell, Jr.

Satterlee, Helen Laval Dupre (Mrs. J. F.)

Satterlee, John Franklin

Satterlee, Mary Capers (Mrs. Chas.)

Saussy, Florence Perry (Mrs. G. S.)

Saussy, George Stone

Saussy, George Stone, Jr.

Saye, Carolyn McCants (Mrs. W. E.)

Saye, Wilbourne Earle

Saye, Wilbourne Earle, Jr.

Schellenberg, Corinne

Schellenberg, Ingeborg

Schirmer, Josephine Jackson (Mrs. F. M.)

Schmidt, Charles Miles

Scott, Lemuel Wardlaw, Jr.

Seabrook, Cotesworth Pinckney

Seabrook, Cotesworth Pinckney, Jr.

Seabrook, Ellen Childs

Seabrook, Mary Thomas Childs (Mrs. C. P.)

Seabrook, Robert Childs

Sears, Irma May

Sears, Van Alden

Seay, Milo Berry

Seibels, Bertha Willingham (Mrs. J. J.)

Seibels, Calder Willingham

Seibels, Edwin Grenville

Seibels, Edwin Grenville, II

Seibels, Hugh Thompson

Seibels, John Jacob

Seibels, Robert Emmett

Seibels, Robert Emmett, Jr.

Selby, Alice

Selby, Anna Knight (Mrs. G. A.)

Selby, Gilbert Augustus

Shafto, Godfrey Richard

Shafto, Treva Hanson (Mrs. G. R.)

Shand, Gadsden Edwards

Shand, Julian Bonham

Shand, Louly

Shand, Lucy McDonald (Mrs. J. B.)

Shand, Mary Wright

Shand, Mary Wright

Shand, Patience Bonham (Mrs. G. E.)

Shand, Selina Coles (Mrs. W. M.)

Shand, William Munro

Shand, William Munro, Jr.

Shinn, John Beach, Jr.

Shinn, Minnie Hughes Rogers (Mrs. J. B., Jr.)

Shockley, Dorothy Austin (Mrs. C. G.)

Simon, Mitry

Simon, Nazha (Mrs. Mitry)

Simpkins, Jennie Wardlaw

Simpkins, John Elliott, Jr.

Simpkins, Sarah Lewis (Mrs. McG.)

Simpson, Mary Bond Screven (Mrs. W. M.)

Simpson, Mary Bond Screven

Simpson, William Crayton

Sims, James Farr

Sims, Ramelle Heriot (Mrs. J. F., Sr.)

Sims, Reba Hiers (Mrs. J. F.)

Sims, Walter Heriot

Singleton, Myrtis Malpass (Mrs. Rich.)

Singleton, Richard

Siokos, Amelia Sabbagha (Mrs. Z. J.)

Siokos, Badeia Sabbagha (Mrs. J. C.)

Sloan, Allan Poe

Sloan, Earle Wattrus (Mrs. R. B.)

Sloan, Frances Blake (Mrs. J. T., Sr.)

Sloan, Frances Blake

Sloan, Isabel Whaley (Mrs. J. T.)

Sloan, John Trimmier

Sloan, John Trimmier, Jr.

Sloan, Lessie Dwight (Mrs. A. P.)

Sloan, Robert Beverley

Smith, James Arthur

Smith, Mary Walker Pringle (Mrs. H. A.)

Snowden, Annie W o r l e y (Mrs. Yates)

Snowden, Lucy Lydia Worley (Mrs. Thos. H.)

Sparkman, Frances Harrison (Mrs. S. T., Sr.)

Sparkman, Nora Harrison

Sparks, Susan Guignard (Mrs. S. G.)

Spong, Ernest Maye

Spong, Katherine Blakeney (Mrs. E. M.)

Starling, Harvey Right (deceased)

Starling, Roberta Cowan Hatch (Mrs. H. R.)

Stephan, Virginia Taylor Lewis (Mrs. R. M.)

Stolz, Irwin William

Stolz, Sarah Fisher (Mrs. I. W.)

Stoney, Samuel Reed

Strickland, Leone Dexter

Strickland, Ray Pou (Mrs. T. S.)

Strickland, Taylor Starling

Stuart, Ellen Elliott

Summer, Louise Carter (Mrs. W. C.)

Summer, William Carl

Sumner, George Vibert

Sumner, Letitia Sybil (Mrs. Ernest, Sr.)

Sumner, Perla Vittoria (Mrs. G. V.)

Sumner, Shirley Geraldine

Sutherland, Evelyn Smith (Mrs. E. S.)

Swaffield, Angel Cheatham (Mrs. F. G.)

Swaffield, Caroline

Swaffield, Frederick Green

Swaffield, Frederick Green, Jr.

Sweeny, Grace Cameron (Mrs. W. O.)

Sweeny, William Oglesby

Sylvan, Frances Elizabeth

Sylvan, Gustaf

Sylvan, Lucile Treadwell (Mrs. Gustaf)

T

Taber, Elizabeth Ray (Mrs. Stephen)

Taber, Molly Geise

Talley, Lilah

Taylor, Alexander Ross

Taylor, Alexander Ross, II

Taylor, Benjamin Walter

Taylor, Celia Foote (Mrs. G. D.)

Taylor, Edward Coles

Taylor, George Dwight

Taylor, Glen Heriot (Mrs. A. E.)

Taylor, Goodwyn Rhett

Taylor, Helen Whaley

Taylor, John

Taylor, Julius Heyward

Taylor, Julius Heyward, Jr.

Taylor, Katherine

Taylor, Margaret Rhett (Mrs. J. H.)

Taylor, Virginia Lee (Mrs. A. R.)

Taylor, Virginia Hayne

Taylor, Willie Sanders (Mrs. J. A.)

Tharin, Lucy Hinnant (Mrs. T. S.)

Tharin, Mabelle Whitney (Mrs. M. W.)

Tharin, Theodore Sherwood

Thomas, Benjamin

Thomas, Caroline Gibbes

Thomas, Elizabeth

Thomas, John Peyre

Thomas, John Waties

Thomas, John Waties, Jr.

Thomas, Louise

Thomas, Mary Shannonhouse (Mrs. J. W.)

Thomas, Mamie

Thomson, Mary Blanchard

Thorne, Martha Bailey (Mrs. R. E.)

Thorne, Robert Eugene

Todd, Beverley Cathcart (Mrs. S. R.)

Todd, Samuel Rutherford

Tompkins, Amelia

Tompkins, Elizabeth Sewel Boykin
(Mrs. F. G., Jr.)
Tompkins, Frank Gary, Jr.
Tompkins, Louise Rook
Townsend, Isabel Welch
Townsend, Willie Miller (Mrs. P.
C.)
Townsend, Philip Clayton
Townsend, Virginia Clayton
Tucker, Alda Stanley (Mrs. J. S.)
Tucker, James Sparkman

U

Urquhart, Alice Childs (Mrs. J. B.)
Urquhart, James Burwell
Urquhart, James Burwell, Jr.

V

Valentine, Edna Simpson
VanBenthuysen, Francis
VanBenthuysen, Lillian   Heath
(Mrs. F.)

W

Wackym, Athalene
Wackym, Mitchell
Wackym, Sophie Ktite (Mrs. A. G.)
Walker, Ashley Perkins
Walker, Ashton
Walker, Cosmo Lowry
Walker, Elizabeth   McIver   L a w
(Mrs. R. B.)
Walker, Elizabeth Whitner
Walker, Eugene Ellison
Walker, Gertrude
Walker, George Rivers Pinckney
Walker, Hattie   McAllister   (Mrs.
A. P.)
Walker, Helen Irving Rion (Mrs. G.
M.)
Walker, Julia Keenan (Mrs. C. L.)
Walker, Julius Henry
Walker, Julius Henry, Jr.
Walker, Marjorie Ellison (Mrs. J.
H.)

Walker, Mary Ross Seibels (Mrs.
G. R. P.)
Walker, Mary Sabra (deceased)
Walker, Nannie Virgilia (Mrs. J.
F.)
Walker, Robert Bratton
Wallace, Alfred
Wallace, Frances
Wallace, James Mayrant
Wallace, James Mayrant, Jr.
Wallace, Louise Adams
Walsh, Genevieve McCaw (Mrs. K.)
Walsh, Henrietta Ellen
Wannamaker, William Elliott
Wardlaw, Albert Lee
Wardlaw, Leila Stuart Elliott (Mrs.
A. L.)
Waring, Clark DuVal
Waring, Florence Yarborough (Mrs.
C. D.)
Waring, Minnehaha (Mrs. R. S.)
Waring, Robert Stuart
Washington, Charlotte Garnett
Waterfall, Charles Hardy
Waterfall,   Katherine   FitzSimons
(Mrs. C. H.)
Waters, Agnes Seibels (Mrs. T. W.)
Waties, Katherine Calhoun
Watson, Henry Shorter
Watson, Henry Shorter, Jr.
Watson, Katherine Frasier (Mrs.
H. S.)
Watts, Marie   Elizabeth   Moultrie
(Mrs. H. F. B.)
Watts, Holt Fairfield Butt
Webber, Rebecca Salley (Mrs. C.
P.)
Weissinger, Sallie Daniel (Mrs. G.
L.)
Weissinger, Helen
Weston, Alma Daniel (Mrs. T. I.)
Weston, Elizabeth V a n d e r h o r s t
(Mrs. Wm.)
Weston, Florence   T u c k e r   (Mrs.
Wm., II)
Weston, Henrietta   Nelson   (Mrs.
Wm., Jr.)
Weston, William

Weston, Wm., Jr.
Whaley, Alys Cathcart
Whaley, Edna Reed (Mrs. M. S.)
Whaley, Marcellus Seabrook
Williams, Agnes Geralyn
Williams, Agnes Tompkins (Mrs. T. C.)
Williams, Carolyn Elizabeth
Williams, Thomas Clay
Wilson, Adeline Selby (Mrs. C. C.)
Wingfield, Elizabeth McCreery (Mrs. E. L., Sr.)
Wingfield, Elizabeth Sherrod
Wingfield, Emmett Lee
Wingfield, Louisa Shand (Mrs. E. L.)
Wingfield, William
Withers, James Heyward

Wright, Elizabeth Marshall (Mrs. E. M.)
Wright, Mary Adams
Wright, Mary Louise Everett (Mrs. T. B.)

Y

Young, Mamie (Mrs. J. A.)
Young, Harold Abner
Young, Lillian Cochran (Mrs. Harold A.)

Z

Zeigler, Wilbur Clifton
Zimmerman, Christie Powers (Mrs. S. J.)